CRESSMAN LIBRARY

CEDAR CREST COLLEGE

Presented by
Drs. Paul and June Schlueter

In Memory of
Dr. Robert C. Williams

Walt Whitman
A Supplementary Bibliography: 1961-1967

THE SERIF SERIES: BIBLIOGRAPHIES AND CHECKLISTS

GENERAL EDITOR: William White, Wayne State University

---

1 *Wilfred Owen (1893-1918): A Bibliography* by William White, with a prefacing note by Harold Owen
SBN: 87338–017–7/ 41pp/ introduction/ preface/ $3.50

2 *Raymond Chandler: A Checklist* by Matthew J. Bruccoli
SBN: 87338–015–0/ ix, 35pp/ introduction/ $3.25

3 *Emily Dickinson, A Bibliography: (1850-1966)* by Sheila T. Clendenning
SBN: 87338–016–9/ xxx, 145pp/ preface/ introduction/ $5.00

4 *John Updike: A Bibliography* by C. Clarke Taylor
SBN: 87338–018–5/ vii, 82pp/ introduction/ $4.25

5 *Walt Whitman: A Supplementary Bibliography (1961-1967)* by James T. F. Tanner
SBN: 87338–019–3/ vi, 59pp/ introduction/ $3.75

6 *Erle Stanley Gardner: A Checklist* by E. H. Mundell
SBN: 87338–034–7/ ix, 91pp/ introduction/ indices/ $5.50

7 *Bernard Malamud: An Annotated Checklist* by Rita Nathalie Kosofsky
SBN: 87338–037–1/ xii, 63pp/ preface/ author's note/ $4.25

8 *Samuel Beckett: A Checklist* by J. F. T. Tanner and J. Don Vann
SBN: 87338–051–7/ vi, 85pp/ introduction/ $4.50

9 *Robert G. Ingersoll: A Checklist* by Gordon Stein
SBN: 87338–047–9/ xxx, 128pp/ preface/ introduction/ index/ $5.00

Walt Whitman

A Supplementary Bibliography: 1961-1967

By James T. F. Tanner
North Texas State University

The Kent State University Press

The Serif Series: Number 5
Bibliographies and Checklists

William White, General Editor
Wayne State University

Second Printing
Library of Congress Card Catalogue Number 67-65586
Standard Book Number 87338-019-3
Manufactured in the United States of America
Designed by Merald E. Wrolstad

First Edition

Introduction

The last important, full length bibliography of works about Walt Whitman, which appeared in 1961, was done by Evie Allison Allen and was included in Gay Wilson Allen's *Walt Whitman As Man, Poet, and Legend.* This excellent bibliography covered the years from 1945 to 1960. My intention in this present compilation is simply to bring up to date, by covering the years 1961-1966, a bibliography of works *about* Walt Whitman.

The student interested in completeness of bibliographical survey may be reasonably well satisfied if he will consult the following bibliographies (listed in chronological order):

Triggs, Oscar Lovell. "Bibliography of Walt Whitman," in *Complete Writings of Walt Whitman.* New York and London: G. P. Putnam's Sons, 1902, X, 139-233.

Holloway, Emory and Saunders, Henry S. "[Bibliography of Walt] Whitman," in *Cambridge History of American Literature.* New York: G. P. Putnam's Sons, 1918, II, 551-581.

Wells, Carolyn and Goldsmith, Alfred F. *A Concise Bibliography of the Works of Walt Whitman.* Boston: Houghton Mifflin and Co., 1922. 107 pp.

Allen, Gay Wilson. *Twenty-Five Years of Walt Whitman Bibliography*—1918-1942. Boston: The F. W. Faxon Co., 1943. 57 pp.

Library of Congress. *Walt Whitman, a Catalog Based Upon the Collections of the Library of Congress with Notes*. Washington, D.C.: Govt. Printing Office, 1955. 147 pp.

Allen, Evie Allison. "A Checklist of Whitman Publications 1945-1960," in Gay Wilson Allen, *Walt Whitman As Man, Poet, and Legend*. Carbondale: Southern Illinois University Press, 1961, pp. 179-244.

In addition, one should consult William White's checklist of Whitman publications appearing quarterly in the *Walt Whitman Review* as well as current lists appearing in such well known journals as *PMLA* and *American Literature*.

The bibliography below is divided into two parts: (1) bibliographies and (2) criticism, biography and reviews. The bibliographies are listed in chronological order; all entries in the second part are listed in alphabetical order with the exception of items appearing under the "Unsigned" designation which are listed chronologically.

I am especially indebted to William White's lists appearing in the *Walt Whitman Review* (incorporated here with permission along with occasional annotations) as well as to other compilers listed below. I wish also to thank the committee on faculty research funds of North Texas State University for making available to me time and some money for completion of this bibliography. Mr. Richard Kelch, my research assistant, has saved me time and frustration by his willingness to work harder than he was supposed to have done. I will appreciate suggestions and comments.

JAMES T. F. TANNER

Denton, Texas

A. Bibliographies

Allen, Evie Allison. "A Checklist of Whitman Publications 1945-1960," in Gay Wilson Allen, *Walt Whitman As Man, Poet, and Legend*. Carbondale: Southern Illinois University Press, 1961, pp. 179-244.

Dyson, May. "Index, *The Walt Whitman Birthplace Bulletin*, Volumes I-IV, October 1957 to July 1961," *Walt Whitman Birthplace Bulletin*, IV (July 1961), 30-32.

Grant, Rena. "The Livezey-Whitman Manuscripts," *Walt Whitman Review*, VII (March 1961), 3-14.

Mummendey, Richard. *Belle{s} Lettres of the United States of America in German Translations: A Bibliogrophy*. Bonn: H. Bouvier & Co.; Charlottesville: Bibliographical Society of the University of Virginia, 1961, pp. 179-180.

Stovall, Floyd. *Walt Whitman: Representative Selections, with Introduction, Bibliography, and Notes*. Revised Edition. American Century Series. New York: Hill and Wang, 1961.

White, William. "Whitman: A Current Bibliography," *Walt Whitman Review*, VII (March, June, September, December 1961), 16-18, 38, 57-59, 78-79.

Faner, Robert D. "Whitman on Records," *Walt Whitman Review*, VIII (June 1962) 33-38.

White, William. "Whitman: A Current Bibliography," *Walt*

Whitman Review, VIII (March, June, September, December 1962), 22-23, 46-47, 71, 94-95.

Woodward, Robert H. "Whitman on Records: Addenda," *Walt Whitman Review*, VIII (December 1962), 91-92. [See Faner, above.]

Michel, Pierre. "Whitman Revisited," *Revue des Langues vivantes*, XXIX (January-February 1963), 79-83. [On recent books about Whitman.]

Neilson, Kenneth P. *The World of Walt Whitman Music: A Bibliographical Study*. Hollis, Queensboro, Long Island, N. Y.: The Author, 1963. iv, 144 pp.

Thorp, Willard. "Whitman," in *Eight American Authors: A Review of Research and Criticism*, edited by Floyd Stovall, *et. als.* New York: W. W. Norton & Co., Inc., 1963, pp. 271-318.

White, William. "Whitman: A Current Bibliography," *Walt Whitman Review*, I X(March, June, September, December 1963), 21, 45, 70, 93-94. [December list with P. V. Rizzo.]

Corwin, Susan A. *Hawthorne to Hemingway: An Annotated Bibliography of Books From 1945 to 1963 About Nine American Writers*. Edited by Robert H. Woodward. San Jose, Calif.: San Jose State College, 1964, pp. 17-27.

White, William. "Whitman: A Current Bibliography," *Walt Whitman Review*, X (June, September, December 1964), 46-67 (with P. V. Rizzo), 77-78 ,102-103.

Libman, V. A. "Bibliography: Critical Works on American Literature in Russia. . . Walt Whitman," *Problems in the History of the Literature of the U.S.A.* Edited by G. P. Zlobin. Moscow, 1964, pp. 460-463. [In Cyrillic.]

Miller, F. DeWolfe. "Whitman Bibliography in Russia," *Walt Whitman Review*, XI (September 1965), 77-79.

White, William. "*Walt Whitman Review*, Index Vols. VI-X, March 1960-December 1964," *Walt Whitman Review*, XI (March 1965), i-vii [insert].

————. "Whitman: A Current Bibliography," *Walt Whitman Review*, XI (March, June, September, December 1965), 21-23, 56-57, 80-81, 104-105.

————. "Whitman: A Current Bibliography," *Walt Whitman Review*, XII (March, June, September, December 1966), 22, 45-46, 102-103.

Woodbridge, Hensley C. "Walt Whitman: Additional Bibliography in Spanish," *Walt Whitman Review*, XII (September 1966), 70-71. [Supplements Fernando Alegría's *Walt Whitman en Hispanoamerica*, 1954.]

B. Criticism, Biography, and Reviews

A, J. N. Review of William Coyle, *The Poet and the President: Whitman's Lincoln Poems, Journal of the State Historical Society*, LV (Autumn 1962), 315.

Abel, Darrel. "Walt Whitman, 1819-1892," in *American Literature*. Great Neck, New York: Barron's Educational Series, Inc., 1963, II, 451-498.

Adams, Richard P. "The Apprenticeship of William Faulkner," *Tulane Studies in English*, XII (1962), 113-156.

Adolorata, Sister Mary, O.S.M., ed. *The Growing Years of American Literature*. New York: The Macmillan Co., 1961, pp. 3-27.

Ahlers, Alice. "Cinematographic Technique in *Leaves of Grass*," *Walt Whitman Review*, XII (December 1966), 93-97.

Ahnebrink, Lars. Review of Douglas Grant, *Walt Whitman and His English Admirers*, *Studia Neophilologica*, XXXV (1963), 170.

Allen, Gay Wilson. "Asselineau's Study in English," *Walt Whitman Review*, IX (March 1963), 19-20. [Review of Roger Asselineau, *The Evolution of Walt Whitman*, Vols. I and II.]

———. "Editing the Writings of Walt Whitman: A Million Dollar Project without a Million Dollars," *Arts and Sci-*

ences (New York University), [No. 2] (Winter 1962-63), pp. 7-12.

―――. "A Note on Comparing Whitman and Nietzsche," *Walt Whitman Review*, XI (September 1965), 74-76.

―――. "The Problem of Metaphor in Translating Walt Whitman's 'Leaves of Grass,'" *English Studies Today* (Bern), Second Series, 1961, pp. 269-280.

―――. Review of C. N. Stavrou, *Whitman and Nietzsche: A Comparative Study of Their Thought*, *American Literature*, XXXVII (November 1965), 3-6.

―――. "Songs of Himself," *Saturday Review*, XLVII (27 February 1965), 47-48 [Review of Horace Traubel, *With Walt Whitman in Camden*, Vol. V.]

―――. *Walt Whitman*. Evergreen Profile Book 19. New York: Grove Press, Inc., London: Evergreen Books Ltd., 1961. 192 pp.

―――. *Walt Whitman As Man, Poet, and Legend*. Carbondale: Southern Illinois University Press, 1961.

―――. "Walt Whitman Edition Silently Progressing," *The Long-Islander*, 26 May 1966, Section II, p. 5.

―――. *Walt Whitman in Selbstzeugnissen und Bildokumenten*. Dargestellt von Gay Wilson Allen. Rowohlts Monographien Nr. 66. Hamburg: Rowoholt, 1962. 177 pp. [German translation of 1961 Grove Press *Walt Whitman*.]

―――. "Whitman: Cosmos Inspired," *The Long-Islander*, 25 May 1961, Section III, p. 1.

―――. "With Walt at the Front," *New York Times Book Review*, LXVI (22 January 1961), 3. [Review of Walter Lowenfels, *Walt Whitman's Civil War*, and Roger Asselineau, *The Evolution of Walt Whitman*.]

Arden, Eugene. "The Walt Whitman Colloquium: Foreword," *Long Island University Journal*, I (June 1966), 3-4.

Askew, Melvin W. "Whitman's 'As I Ebb'd with the Ocean of Life,'" *Walt Whitman Review*, X (December 1964), 87-92.

Aspiz, Harold. "Unfolding the Folds," *Walt Whitman Review*, XII (December 1966), 81-87.

Asselineau, Roger. "African Leaves of Grass," *The Long-Islander*, 26 May 1966, Section II, p. 5.

————. "If Walt Lived Today," *American Dialog*, II (October-November 1965), 3-6.

————. "A Poet's Dilemma: Walt Whitman's Attitude to Literary History and Literary Criticism," in *Literary History & Literary Criticism: Acta of the Ninth Congress International Federation of Modern Language and Literature*, Held at New York City August 25 to 31, 1963. Edited by Leon Edel, Kenneth McKee, and William Gibson, co-editors. New York University Press, 1965 [copyright 1964] pp. 50-64.

————. Review of Charles R. Metzger, *Thoreau and Whitman: A Study of Their Esthetics*, *Archiv fur des Studium der neureren Sprachen und Literaturen*, CXV (April 1963), 71-72.

————. Review of Gay Wilson Allen, *Walt Whitman* and *Walt Whitman As Man, Poet, and Legend*, *Revue de Littérature comparée*, XXXVII (July-September 1963), 473-475.

————. Review of Gay Wilson Allen, *Walt Whitman As Man, Poet, and Legend*, *Etudes anglaises*, XVI (January-March 1963), 98-99.

Atkinson, Brooks. Review of Walter Lowenfels, *Walt Whit-*

man's Civil War, San Francisco Chronicle, 15 January 1961, p. 28.

Avery, Jewell. "Reverie at Piney Woods," *The Pine Torch*, XXVI (July-August-September 1964), 4. [An 11th grade student relates *Leaves of Grass* to her own life in Piney Woods, Mississippi.)

Azarnoff, Roy S. "Walt Whitman's Concept of the Oratorical Ideal," *Quarterly Journal of Speech*, XLVII (April 1961), 169-172.

――――. "Walt Whitman's Lecture on Lincoln in Haddonfield," *Walt Whitman Review*, IX (September 1963), 65-66.

Barnshaw, Harold D. "Walt Whitman's Physicians in Camden," *Transactions and Studies of the College of Physicians of Philadelphia*, 4th Series, XXXI (January, 1964), 227-230.

Basler, Roy P., ed. *Walt Whitman's Memoranda During the War & Death of Abraham Lincoln.* Reproduced in Facsimile. Bloomington: Indiana University Press, 1962.

Baylet, Joseph O. and Holland, Robert B. "Whitman, W. T. Snead, and the Pall Mall Gazette: 1886-1887," *American Literature*, XXXIII (March 1961), 68-72.

Berger, Art. "Walt's Sons Speak," *American Dialog*, II (October-November 1965), 6-8.

Bernbrock, John, S.J. "George H. Colton, Whitman, and 'By Blue Ontario's Shore,'" *Walt Whitman Review*, VIII (June 1962), 38-40.

――――. "Walt Whitman and 'Anglo-Saxonism,'" *Dissertation Abstracts*, XXII (1962), 2789-2790.

Bertholf, Robert J. "Poetic Epistemology of Whitman's 'Out of the Cradle,'" *Walt Whitman Review*, X (September 1964), 73-77.

Betsky, Seymour. "Whose Walt Whitman?: French Scholars and American Critics," *English Studies*, XLVII (June 1966), 199-208.

Black, Colin M. "Walt Whitman 'Fancied' the Navesink," *Asbury Park* [New Jersey] *Sunday Press*, 12 August 1962, p. 14.

Blackwell, Louise. " 'Song of Myself' and the Organic Theory of Poetry," *Walt Whitman Review*, XII (June 1966), 35-41.

Blodgett, Harold, ed. (with Sculley Bradley). *Leaves of Grass: Comprehensive Reader's Edition. The Collected Writings of Walt Whitman*. New York University Press, 1965.

————. "*Leaves of Grass* in Iran: Two Episodes," *The Long-Islander*, 25 May 1961, Section III, p. 1.

————. "A Poet's Hero," *Union College Symposium*, I (Spring 1962), 28-31. [On the Whitman-Lincoln relationship.]

————. Review of Emory Holloway, *Free and Lonesome Heart: The Secret of Walt Whitman. South Atlantic Quarterly*, LX (Winter 1961), 116-117.

————. Review of Geoffrey Dutton, *Whitman, American Literature*, XXXIV (November 1962), 442-443.

————. Review of Horace Traubel, *With Walt Whitman in Camden*, Vol. V, *South Atlantic Quarterly*, LXV (Winter 1966), 152-153.

————. Review of Roger Asselineau, *The Evolution of Walt Whitman, Modern Philology*, LIX (November 1961), 144-146.

————. Review of Roger Asselineau, *The Evolution of Walt*

Whitman, Vol. II, *South Atlantic Quarterly*, LXII (Summer 1963), 443-444.

———. Review of Roger Asselineau, *The Evolution of Walt Whitman*, *South Atlantic Quarterly*, LX (Summer 1961), 350-351.

———. "Whitman's Whisperings," *Walt Whitman Review*, VIII (March 1962), 12-16.

———. "Who Listens to Whitman Today?" *Long Island University Journal*, I (March 1966), 28-30.

———. "Who Listens to Whitman Today?" *The Long-Islander*, No. 48 (1965), Sec. II, pp. 4-5.

Bloom, Harold. "The Central Man: Emerson, Whitman, Wallace Stevens," *Massachusetts Review*, VII (Winter 1966), 23-42.

Bluestein, Gene. "The Advantages of Barbarism: Herder and Whitman's Nationalism," *Journal of the History of Ideas*, XXIV (1963), 115-126.

Bode, Carl. "Thoreau's and Whitman's Esthetics," *Walt Whitman Review*, VIII (June 1962), 43-44. [Review of Charles R. Metzger, *Thoreau and Whitman: A Study of Their Esthetics.*]

Borges, Jorge Luis. "The Achievements of Walt Whitman," *Texas Quarterly*, V (Spring 1962), 43-48.

Bracker, Jon. "The Christopher Morley Collection," *Library Chronicle*, VII (1962), 15-19, 35.

———. "The Conclusion of 'Song of Myself,' " *Walt Whitman Review*, X (March 1964), 21-22.

Bradley, E. Sculley, ed. Annual Whitman Anniversary Page. *The Long-Islander*, 28 May 1964, Sec. III, p. 1.

———, ed. (with Harold W. Blodgett). *Leaves of Grass: Comprehensive Reader's Edition. The Collected Writings of Walt Whitman*. New York University Press, 1965.

————. Review of Charles R. Metzger, *Thoreau and Whitman: A Study of Their Esthetics*, *American Literature*, XXXV (May 1963), 245-246.

————. "The Teaching of Whitman," *College English*, XXIII (May 1962), 618-622.

————. "Whitman and Today's Crisis," *The Long-Islander*, No. 48 (1965), Sec. II, pp. 4-5.

————. "Whitman on J. Q. Adams: A Review," *Walt Whitman Review*, VIII (March 1962), 19-20. [Review of Walt Whitman, *The People and John Quincy Adams*.]

Bradley, Van Allen. " 'Even Rarer' Whitman Book Contains His War Memories," *The State Journal* (Lansing, Michigan), 29 July 1962, p. B-10. [Review of Roy P. Basler, *Walt Whitman's Memoranda During the War*.]

Brasher, Thomas L., ed. *The Early Poems and the Fiction*. With Introd. and Notes. *The Collected Writings of Walt Whitman*. New York University Press, 1963.

————. "Whitman's Fiction: Recollections of Long Island," *The Long-Islander*, 28 May 1964, Sec. III, p. 1.

Braun, Sidney D. *"Leaves of Grass* in French," *Walt Whitman Review*, XII (December 1966), 101-102. [Review of *Walt Whitman: Ses meilleures Pages Traduites de l'Anglais*, par Rosaire Dion-Lévesque.]

Brenner, George A. "Whitman and You: Two Human Beings," *Nassau Review*, I (Spring 1965), 84-98.

Bridgman, Richard. "Whitman's Calendar Leaves," *College English*, XXV (March 1964), 420-425.

Bristol, James. "Literary Criticism in Specimen Days," *Walt Whitman Review*, XII (March 1966), 16-19.

Broderick, John C. "An Unpublished Whitman Letter and Other Manuscripts," *American Literature*, XXXVII (January 1966), 475-478.

————, ed. *Whitman the Poet: Materials for Study*. Belmont, California: Wadsworth Publishing Company, Inc., 1962. xiv, 186 pp.

Brown, Clarence A. Review of *The Correspondence of Walt Whitman*, Vols. I and II, *American Quarterly*, XIV (Fall 1962), 510-511.

————. Review of Walt Whitman, *The Correspondence*: Vol. III, 1876-1885, edited by Edwin Haviland Miller; and *Prose Works 1892: Vol. II, Collect and Other Prose*, edited by Floyd Stovall, *American Quarterly*, XVI (Fall 1964), 501-502.

————. Review of Walt Whitman, *The Early Poems and the Fiction*, edited by Thomas L. Brasher; and *Prose Works 1892: Volume I, Specimen Days*, edited by Floyd Stovall, *American Quarterly*, XV (Winter 1963), 596-597.

————. "Walt Whitman and 'The New Poetry,'" *American Literature*, XXXIII (March 1961), 33-45.

Bryson, George S. "Walt Whitman," *New York Times Book Review*, 15 May 1966, p. 32. [On Whitman in Laurel Springs, New Jersey, where he stayed weekends in the Stafford farmhouse, now an historical shrine.]

Budd, Louis J. Review of Gay Wilson Allen, *Walt Whitman*, *South Atlantic Quarterly*, LX (Autumn 1961), 513.

Byron, John E. "Significance of T, I, and O in 'Crossing Brooklyn Ferry,'" *Walt Whitman Review*, IX (December 1963), 89-90.

Cadden, John O'Shea, ed. "Whitman Issue," *Nassau Review*, I (Spring 1965), i-iv, 1-118.

Cady, Edwin H. "The 1860 Leaves in Facsimile," *Walt Whitman Review*, VIII (June 1962), 41-43. [Review of Walt Whitman, *Leaves of Grass: Facsimile Edition of the 1860 Text*, with an Introduction by Roy Harvey Pearce.]

Cambon, Glauco. *La Lotta con Proteo*. Milano: Bompiani, 1963.

Cameron, Kenneth Walter. "Redpath Writes Whitman on the Transcendentalists," *Emerson Society Quarterly*, No. 29 (IV Quarter 1962), pp. 21-26.

Cardwell, Guy A. Review of *The Correspondence of Walt Whitman*, Vols. I and II, *The Key Reporter* (Phi Beta Kappa), XXVII (Winter 1961-62), 5.

Cargill, Oscar. "Walt Whitman and Civil Rights," *Long Island University Journal*, I (June 1966), 20-27.

Carlisle, Ervin F. *"Leaves of Grass*: Whitman's Epic Drama of the Soul and I." Ph.D. Dissertation, Indiana, 1963. [See *Dissertation Abstracts*, XXIV (1964), 3727-3728.]

Carpenter, Frederic I. "A Hindu Interpretation—and More," *Walt Whitman Review*, IX (September 1965), 79-80. [Review of V. K. Chari, *Whitman in the Light of Vendantic Mysticism: An Interpretation*.]

Chari, V. K. "Structure and Poetic Growth in *Leaves of Grass*," *Walt Whitman Review*, IX (September, 1963), 58-63.

————. "Whitman and the Beat Poets," *Emerson Society Quarterly*, No. 39 (II Quarter 1965), 34-37.

————. *Whitman in the Light of Vedantic Mysticism: An Interpretation*. Foreword by Gay Wilson Allen. Lincoln: University of Nebraska Press, 1965. xvi, 208 pp.

Chase, Richard. "Artfully Artless Letters of a 'Rough,'" *New York Times Book Review*, LXVI (2 July 1961), 5. [Review of Walt Whitman, *The Correspondence*, Vols. I and II, edited by Edwin Haviland Miller.]

————. *Walt Whitman*. University of Minnesota Pamphlets on American Writers No. 9. Minneapolis: University of Minnesota Press, 1961.

Chatman, Vernon V., III. "Figures of Repetition in Whitman's 'Songs of Parting,'" *Bulletin of the New York Public Library*, LXIX (February 1965), 77-82.

Christ, Ronald. "Walt Whitman: Image and Credo," *American Quarterly*, XVII (Spring 1965), 92-103.

Christman, Henry M., ed. *Walt Whitman's New York from Manhattan to Montauk*. New York: The Macmillan Co.; London: Collier Macmillan Limited, 1963. 188 pp.

Clare, Sister Miriam, O.S.F. "The Sea and Death in *Leaves of Grass*," *Walt Whitman Review*, X (March 1964), 14-16.

Cobb, Robert P. "Whitman as Hospital Visitor," *Emerson Society Quarterly*, No. 22 (I Quarter 1961), 3-5.

Coberly, James H. "Whitman's 'Children of Adam' Poems," *Emerson Society Quarterly*, No. 22 (I Quarter 1961), 5-8.

Coffman, Stanley K., Jr. "The World Dimensional in the Poetry of *Leaves of Grass*," *Emerson Society Quarterly*, No. 22 (I Quarter 1961), 8-10.

Cohen, Marvin. *A Comprehensive Outline of Whitman's Leaves of Grass*. East Longmeadow, Mass.: Harvard Outline Company, 1965. 44 pp.

Collins, Christopher. "The Uses of Observation: A Study of Correspondental Vision in the Writings of Emerson, Thoreau, and Whitman." Ph.D. dissertation, Columbia, 1964. [*See Dissertation Abstracts*, XXVI (1965), 352.]

————. "Whitman's Open Road and Where It Led," *Nassau Review*, I (Spring 1965), 101-110.

Collins, Margaret B. "Walt Whitman Ghost Writer for James Speed?" *Filson Club History Quarterly*, XXXVII (October 1963), 305-324.

Colombo, J. R. *Richard Maurice Bucke: Catalogue to the Exhi-*

bition, June 10-14, 1963, Toronto. University of Toronto Press, 20 pp.

Cook, Raymond A. "Empathic Identification in 'Song of Myself,': A Key to Whitman's Poetry," *Walt Whitman Review*, X (March 1964), 3-10.

————. Review of Emory Holloway, *Free and Lonesome Heart: The Secret of Walt Whitman, Georgia Review*, XV (Spring 1961), 113-114.

Cooper, Reuben. "Whitman and Dostoievski: The Horns of a Dilemma," *The Torch*, XXXVI (January 1963), 13-18.

Cox, James M. "Walt Whitman, Mark Twain, and the Civil War," *Sewanee Review*, LXIX (1961), 187-193.

Coyle, William. *The Poet and the President: Whitman's Lincoln Poems.* New York: The Odyssey Press, Inc., 1962. xiii, 334 pp.

Daiches, David. "Geoffrey Dutton's Whitman," *Walt Whitman Review*, IX (June 1963), 43-44.

————. "Imagery and Mood in Tennyson and Whitman," *English Studies Today* (Bern), Second Series, 1961, pp. 217-232.

Daugherty, James. *Walt Whitman's America.* Cleveland and New York: The World Publishing Co., 1964. 111 pp.

Davenport, John L. "Birthplace Association Honors Oscar Lion," *The Long-Islander*, 26 May 1966, Section II, p. 5.

————. "*Leaves of Grass*: Walt Whitman's Salute 'To You,' " *Nassau Review*, I (Spring 1965), 81-83.

————. "A Presentation to Oscar Lion," *Long Island University Journal*, I (June 1966), 18-19.

Davidson, James. "Whitman's 'Twenty-Eight Young Men,' " *Walt Whitman Review*, XII (December 1966), 100-101.

Davies, Phillips G. "A Discovery of Death," *CEA Critic*,

XXVII (May 1965), 7-8. [Gerard Manley Hopkins and Whitman.]

Davis, Charles T. "Letters from the Old Hawk," *Nation*, CXCIII (15 July 1961), 34-35. [Review of *The Correspondence of Walt Whitman*, Vols. I and II, edited by Edwin Haviland Miller.]

————. "Walt Whitman and the Problem of an American Tradition," *CLA Journal*, V (September 1961), 1-16.

Deer, Irving. Review of Roger Asselineau, *The Evolution of Walt Whitman: The Creation of a Personality*, *Quarterly Journal of Speech*, XLVII (April 1961), 206.

DeFalco, Joseph M. "The Narrative Shift in Whitman's 'Song of Myself,' " *Walt Whitman Review*, IX (December 1963), 82-84.

De Koven, Bernard. "A 'Symphonic' Arrangement of Two Whitman Poems," introduced by Sholom J. Kahn, *Walt Whitman Review*, IX (June 1963), 37-40.

Detweiler, Robert. "The Concrete Universal in Democratic Vistas," *Walt Whitman Review*, IX (June 1963), 40-41.

Dion-Lévesque, Rosaire. *Walt Whitman: Ses meilleures Pages Traduites de l'Anglais*. Québec: Les Presses de l'Université Laval, 1965. 242 pp.

Dobel, Ken. *Walt Whitman and the Kid in the Woodshed: A Collection of Poems and Poem-Plays*. Torrance, Calif.: Hors Commerce Press, 1966. 44 pp.

Donald, David. Review of Roy P. Basler, ed., *Walt Whitman's Memoranda During the War & Death of Abraham Lincoln*, *Lincoln Herald*, LXIV (Summer 1962), 102.

Doyle, P. A. "The Walt Whitman Exhibit at Nassau Community College Library," *Library Newsletter* (Nassau Community College, Garden City, New York), I (May 1966), 1-4.

Duerksen, Roland A. "Shelley's 'Defence' and Whitman's 1855 'Preface': A Comparison," *Walt Whitman Review*, X (September 1964), 51-60.

Duffey, Bernard. "An Idea of Poetry," *Poetry*, CVII (March 1966), 397-399. [Review of Walt Whitman, *Leaves of Grass: Comprehensive Reader's Edition.*]

————. "Romantic Coherence and Incoherence in American Poetry, Part II [Whitman and Melville]," *Centenniel Review*, VIII (Fall 1964), 453-464.

Dutton, Geoffrey. *Whitman.* New York: Grove Press, Inc.; Edinburgh: Oliver and Boyd Ltd., 1961. 120 pp. [Reprinted by Barnes & Noble, Writers and Critics Series, 1966.]

Dyson, Verne. " 'Good Bye My Fancy'—and the Bulletin," *Walt Whitman Birthplace Bulletin*, IV (July 1961), 13-15.

————. "The Story of Walt Whitman House," *Walt Whitman Birthplace Bulletin*, IV (July 1961), 15-27. [From his book, *Whitmanland.*]

————. "Walt Whitman and the Butterfly," *Walt Whitman Birthplace Bulletin*, IV (April 1961), 3-6.

Ebbets, Benjamin T. "Lunched with Whitman," *Long Island Forum*, XXIX (January 1966), 3.

Eby, E. H. Review of Roger Asselineau, *The Evolution of Walt Whitman*, *Modern Language Quarterly*, XXII (December 1961), 405.

————. Review of James E. Miller, Jr., ed., *Whitman's Song of Myself—Origin, Growth, Meaning, College Composition and Communication*, XVI (February 1965), 54.

————. "Walt Whitman and the Tree of Life," *Walt Whitman Review*, VII (September 1961), 43-51.

————. "Walt Whitman's 'Indirections,' " *Walt Whitman Review*, XII (March 1966), 5-16.

Eckley, Wilton. "Whitman's 'A Noiseless Patient Spider,'" *The Explicator*, XXII (November 1963), Item 20.

Elledge, W. P. "Whitman's 'Lilacs' As Romantic Narrative," *Walt Whitman Review*, XII (September 1966), 59-67.

Fabre, Michel. "Walt Whitman and the Rebel Poets: A Note on Whitman's Reputation among Radical Writers during the Depression," *Walt Whitman Review*, XII (December 1966), 88-93.

Faner, Robert D. Review of Walt Whitman, *Leaves of Grass: Comprehensive Reader's Edition*, edited by Harold W. Blodgett and Sculley Bradley, *American Literature*, XXXVII (November 1965), 331-332.

————. "The Use of Primary Source Materials in Whitman Study," *Emerson Society Quarterly*, No. 22 (I Quarter 1961), pp. 10-12.

Feinberg, Charles E. "Adventures in Book Collecting," *Among Friends* (Detroit Public Library), No. 26 (Spring 1962), pp. 1-6.

————. "The Million and First Book in the University of Kentucky Library: The First Edition of Walt Whitman's *Leaves of Grass*, a Gift of the Library Associates," *Keepsake Number 11*, University of Kentucky Library Associates, 1963, 4 pp and insert.

————. "Walt Whitman and His Doctors," *The Long-Islander*, 28 May 1964, Section 3, p. 1.

————. "Walt Whitman and His Doctors," *Archives of Internal Medicine*, CXIV (December 1964), 834-842.

————. "Walt Whitman, Spokesman for Democracy," *Friends of Milner Library* (Illinois State Normal University), XI [1962], 3-12.

————. "Walt Whitman: Yesterday, Today and Tomorrow," *Nassau Review*, I (Spring 1965), 1-18.

————. [Whitman Envelopes to Peter Doyle], *Antiquarian Bookman*, XXXIV (17 August 1964), 587.

Felheim, Marvin. "The Problem of Structure in Some Poems by Whitman," *Aspects of American Poetry: Essays Presented to Howard Mumford*, edited by Richard M. Ludwig. Columbus: Ohio State University Press, 1962, pp. 79-97.

Finkel, William Leo. "Charles Kent's 'Most Affectionate and Overflowing Tribute to Whitman's Great Gifts,' " *Walt Whitman Review*, XI (March 1965), 3-19.

Fleisher, Frederic. "Walt Whitman i Svensksprakig Litteratur," *Nordisk Tidskrift*, XXXVIII (May 1962), 134-140. [Whitman in Sweden and Finland.]

Forrey, Robert. "Whitman and the Freudians," *Mainstream*, XIV (January 1961), 45-52.

Foster, Steven. "Bergson's 'Intuition' and Whitman's 'Song of Myself,' " *Texas Studies in Literature and Language*, VI (Autumn 1964), 276-287.

Freedman, Florence B. "Caricature in Picture and Verse: Walt Whitman in Vanity Fair, 1860," *Walt Whitman Review*, X (March 1964), 18-19, 23.

————. "A Motion Picture 'First' for Whitman: O'Connor's 'The Carpenter,' " *Walt Whitman Review*, IX (June 1963), 31-33, 48.

————. "New Light on an Old Quarrel: Walt Whitman and William Douglas O'Connor 1872," *Walt Whitman Review*, XI (June 1965), 27-52.

————. "Walt Whitman and the Chicago Fire," *Walt Whitman Review*, XII (June 1966), 43-44.

————. "Whitman against Slavery," *The Long-Islander*, No. 48 (1965), Section II, pp. 4-5.

————. "Whitman's Leaves and O'Connor's Harrington: An

1860 Review," *Walt Whitman Review*, IX (September 1963), 63-65.

Freedman, William A. "Whitman and Morality in the Democratic Republic," *Walt Whitman Review*, VII (September 1961), 53-56.

————. "Whitman's 'The World Below the Brine,' " *Explicator*, XXIII (January 1965), Item 39.

Fussell, Edwin. "Walt Whitman's *Leaves of Grass*," *Frontier: American Literature and the American West*. Princeton: Princeton University Press, 1965, pp. 397-411, *et passim*.

Gargano, James W. "Technique in 'Crossing Brooklyn Ferry': The Everlasting Moment," *Journal of English and Germanic Philology*, LXII (April 1963), 262-269.

Garrison, Joseph M., Jr. "John Burroughs As a Literary Critic: A Study Emphasizing His Treatment of Emerson, Whitman, Thoreau, Carlyle, and Arnold," *Dissertation Abstracts*, XXIII (1963), 3372-73. [Duke.]

George, Frederick J. "Are the 'Beatniks' Offspring of Walt?" *Walt Whitman Birthplace Bulletin*, IV (April 1961), 10-12.

Glicksberg, Charles I. "The Lost Self in Modern Literature," *Personalist*, XLIII (Autumn 1962), 527-538.

————. Review of Walt Whitman, *The Early Poems and the Fiction*, edited by Thomas L. Brasher; and *Prose Works 1892: Volume I, Specimen Days*, edited by Floyd Stovall, *American Literature*, XXXVI (March 1964), 90-92.

————. *Walt Whitman and the Civil War*. A Perpetua Book. New York: A. S. Barnes and Co., Inc., 1963. [A paperback reprint, originally published in 1933.]

Gohdes, Clarence. "Sandburg and Whitman: An Anecdote," *The Long-Islander*, 28 May 1964, Section 3, p. 1.

21

————. "Whitman and the 'Good Old Cause,'" *American Literature*, XXXIV (November 1962), 400-403.

————. "Whitman as 'One of the Roughs,'" *Walt Whitman Review*, VIII (March 1962), 18.

————. "Whitman for Seniors and Whitman for Freshmen," *Walt Whitman Review*, VIII (December 1962), 92-93. [Review of R. W. B. Lewis, ed., *The Presence of Walt Whitman* and John C. Broderick, ed., *Whitman the Poet: Materials for Study*.]

Golden, Arthur, ed. Eighth Annual Walt Whitman Page, *The Long-Islander*, 26 May 1966, Section II, p. 5.

————. "A Glimpse into the Workshop: A Critical Evaluation and Diplomatic Transcription of the 'Blue Book,' Walt Whitman's Annotated Copy of the 1860 Edition of *Leaves of Grass*," *Dissertation Abstracts*, XXIV (1963), 743. [New York University.]

————. "New Light on *Leaves of Grass*: Whitman's Annotated Copy of the 1860 (Third) Edition," *Bulletin of the New York Public Library*, LXIX (May 1965), 283-306.

————. "A Note on a Whitman Holograph Poem," *Papers of the Bibliographical Society of America*, LV (III Quarter 1961), 233-236.

————. "A Recovered Whitman Fair Copy of a 'Drum-Taps' Poem, and a 'Sequel to Drum Taps' Fragment," *Papers of the Bibliographical Society of America*, LIX (IV Quarter 1965), 439-441.

————. "Whitman Discusses His Government Service," *The Long-Islander*, 26 May 1966, Section, II, p. 5.

Goldfarb, Clare R. "The Poet's Role in 'Passage to India,'" *Walt Whitman Review*, VIII (1962), 75-79.

Goodale, David. "Walt Whitman, by Gay Wilson Allen: A

Review," *Walt Whitman Review*, VII (September 1961), 56-57.

————. "Walt Whitman's 'Banner at Day-Break,'" *Huntington Library Quarterly*, XXVI (September 1961), 56-57.

————. "'Wood Odors,'" *Walt Whitman Review*, VIII (March 1962), 17.

Gordan, John D. "New in the Berg Collection: 1959-1961 (Part I)," *Bulletin of the New York Public Library*, LXVII (December 1963), 625-638.

Grant, Douglas. "Walt Whitman—I: The Bird of Freedom"; II: "'Poet of the Modern'"; III: "Walt Whitman and His English Admirers," in *Purpose and Place: Essays on American Writers*. London: Macmillan; New York: St. Martin's Press, 1965, pp. 64-91.

————. *Walt Whitman and His English Admirers*. Leeds: Leeds University Press, 1962. 24 pp.

Grant, Rena V. "The Livezey-Whitman Manuscripts," *Walt Whitman Review*, VII (March 1961), 3-14.

Grier, Edward F. Review of Emory Holloway, *Free and Lonesome Heart*, *American Literature*, XXXIII (March 1961), 85-86.

————. Review of Roger Asselineau, *The Evolution of Walt Whitman: The Creation of A Personality*, *Etudes anglaises*, XIV (October-December 1961), 390.

————. Review of R. W. B. Lewis, ed., *The Presence of Walt Whitman*, *American Literature*, XXXVI (March 1964), 90-92.

————. "Whitman's Attack on the Temperance Movement," *Walt Whitman Newsletter*, IV (1958), 78.

Griffin, Robert J. "Notes on Structural Devices in Whitman's Poetry," *Tennessee Studies in Literature*, VI (1961), 15-24.

⸺. "The Interconnectedness of 'Our Old Feuillage,'" *Walt Whitman Review*, VIII (March 1962), 8-12.

⸺. "Whitman's 'Song of Myself,'" *The Explicator*, XXI (October 1962), Item 16.

⸺. "Whitman's 'This Compost,'" *The Explicator*, XXI (April 1963), Item 63.

Groman, George L. "Whitman and the Progressives," *Long-Islander*, 26 May 1966, Section II, p. 5.

Gross, Elliott B. "'Lesson of the Two Symbols,' An Undiscovered Whitman Poem," *Walt Whitman Review*, XII (December 1966), 77-80.

Gross, Harvey. *Sound and Form in Modern Poetry: A Study of Prosody from Thomas Hardy to Robert Lowell*. Ann Arbor: The University of Michigan Press, 1964, pp. 83-88.

Gross, John. "Guides," *New Statesman*, LXII (29 September 1961), 432-433. [Review of Geoffrey Dutton, *Whitman*.]

Gutiérrez, Fermin Estrella. "Walt Whitman y su mensaje," *Commentario*, no. 29 (1961), pp. 34-48.

Haas, Peter. "Whitman's Debt to Folk Music," *Long-Islander*, 26 May 1966, Section II, p. 5.

Hamlin, William C. "Neither Scholarly Nor Belletristic," *St. Louis Post-Dispatch*, 7 January 1965. [Review of Horace Traubel, *With Walt Whitman in Camden,* Vol. V.]

Hancock, Carla. "Walt Whitman, First Modern Poet," *Christian Science Monitor*, 10 April 1965, p. 8.

Hansen, Chadwick. Review of John C. Broderick, ed., *Whitman the Poet: Materials for Study, College English*, XXV (December 1963), 237.

⸺. "Walt Whitman's 'Song of Myself': Democratic Epic," in *American Renaissance, the History of an Era:*

Essays and Interpretations, edited by George Hendrick. Frankfurt: Diesterweg, 1961, pp. 77-88.

Harbison, Winfred A. "Whitman on Lincoln in Facsimile," *Walt Whitman Review,* VIII (September 1962), 69-70. [Review of Roy P. Basler, *Walt Whitman's Memoranda During the War.*]

Harding, Walter. "James E. Miller's Tusa Walt Whitman," *Walt Whitman Review,* IX (December 1963), 92. [Review]

———— (with Milton Meltzer). *"The Greatest Democrat,"* A *Thoreau Profile.* New York: Thomas Y. Crowell Co., 1962, pp. 245-251.

————. Review of *The Correspondence of Walt Whitman,* Vols. I and II, edited by Edwin Haviland Miller, *Chicago Sunday Tribune,* 9 July 1961, p. 2.

Harris, Frank. *My Life and Loves,* edited by John F. Gallagher. New York: Grove Press, 1963, pp. 169-173. [An eyewitness account of Whitman's Philadelphia lecture on Thomas Paine.]

Harris, Kathryn Montgomery. "Review of *Poems of Walt Whitman: Leaves of Grass,"* selected by Lawrence Clark Powell, *Library Journal,* XC (15 February 1965), 52 (Children's Section).

Harris, Marion. "Nature and Materialism: Fundamentals in Whitman's Epistemology," *Walt Whitman Review,* IX (1963), 85-88.

Hart-Davis, Rupert, ed. *The Letters of Oscar Wilde.* London: Rupert Hart-Davis Ltd.; New York: Harcourt, Brace and World, 1962. [See index.]

Hartman, Sadakichi. "Conversations with Whitman," *Long-Islander,* 30 May 1963.

Hatvary, Dr. George, project editor. *Leaves of Grass: Analytic*

Notes and Criticism. A Study Master Publication. New York: American R. D. M. Corp., 1962.

Havlick, Robert J. Review of Roy P. Basler, *Walt Whitman's Memoranda During the War*, *Library Journal*, LXXVII (August 1962), 2757.

Hay, Stephen N. "Rabindranath Tagore in America," *American Quarterly*, XIV (Fall 1962), 439-463.

Heavill, Sister M. Kathleen, R.S.M. "A Whitmanian Look at Whitman," *Walt Whitman Review*, X (March 1964), 17-18.

Hench, Atcheson L. "Walt Whitman Recollected," *American Notes & Queries*, I (October 1962), 22. [Whitman and Folger McKinsey.]

Hendrick, George. "Newspaper Squibs about Whitman," *Walt Whitman Birthplace Bulletin*, IV (April 1961), 7-9.

————. "Unpublished Notes on Whitman in William Sloane Kennedy's Diary," *American Literature*, XXXIV (May 1962), 279-285.

Herreshoff, David. "Floyd Stovall's Edition of *Collect*," *Walt Whitman Review*, XI (December 1965), 103-104. [Review of Walt Whitman, *Prose Works 1892: Volume II, Collect and Other Prose*, edited by Floyd Stovall.]

Hicks, Granville. Review of Roger Asselineau, *The Evolution of Walt Whitman*, Vol. II, *Saturday Review*, XLVI (15 June 1963), 23.

Hicks, John E. "At 82, He Remembers Boyhood Days in House of Walt Whitman," *Kansas City Times*, 20 February 1963, p. 24.

Hill, Hamlin. Review of *The Correspondence of Walt Whitman*, Vols. I and II, *New Mexico Quarterly*, XXXI (Summer 1961), 177-179.

26

Hindus, Milton. "The Goliad Massacre in 'Song of Myself,'"
Walt Whitman Review, VII (December 1961), 77-78.

———. "Literary Echoes in Whitman's 'Passage to India,'"
Walt Whitman Review, VII (September 1961), 52-53.

———. "Notes toward the Definition of a Typical Poetic Line
in Whitman," *Walt Whitman Review*, IX (1963), 75-
81.

Holland, Robert B., and Baylen, Joseph O. "Whitman, W. T.
Snead, and the *Pall Mall Gazette*: 1886-1887," *American
Literature*, XXXIII (March 1961), 68-72.

Hollingsworth, Marian. "Americanism in Franklin Evans,"
Walt Whitman Review, VIII (December 1962), 88-89.

Hollis, C. Carroll. "Volume Three of the *Correspondence*,"
Walt Whitman Review, X (December 1964), 98-100.
[Review of *The Correspondence*: Volume III, edited by
Edwin Haviland Miller.]

Horgan, Paul. *Songs after Lincoln*. New York: Farrer, Straus
and Giroux, 1965, xiii, 74 pp. [According to "Notes and
Comments," pp. 69-74, nine of the thirty-three poems
were suggested by passages from Whitman or have Whitman parallels.]

Huffstickler, Star. "Walt Whitman as a Precursor of Frederick
Jackson Turner," *Walt Whitman Review*, VIII (March
1962), 3-8.

Hunt, Joel A. "Mann and Whitman: Humaniores Litterae,"
Comparative Literature, XIV (1962), 266-271.

Huntley, Frank L. "Walt Whitman and the Death of John F.
Kennedy," *The East-West Review* (Doshisha University,
Kyoto, Japan), I (Spring 1964), 79-85. [Largely on
"When Lilacs Last in the Dooryard Bloom'd."]

Isaacs, Neil D. "The Autoerotic Metaphor in Joyce, Sterne,

Lawrence, Stevens, and Whitman," *Literature and Psychology*, XV (1965), 92-106.

Iwagaki, Morihike. "Walt Whitman," *Kamereon*, No. 5 (Autume 1962), 26-37. [In Japanese.]

Jeffares, A. Norman. "Whitman: The Barbaric Yawp," in *The Great Experiment in American Literature: Six Lectures*, edited by Carl Bode. New York: Frederick A. Praeger, 1961, pp. 29-49.

Jensen, Millie D. "Whitman and Hegel: The Curious Triplicate Process," *Walt Whitman Review*, X (June, 1964), 27-34.

Johannsen, Robert W. Review of Walter Lowenfels, *Walt Whitman's Civil War*, *Journal of Southern History*, XXVIII (February 1962), 104.

[Johnson, Lyndon B.] Reference to Whitman in Signing The Library Service and Construction Act, *Antiquarian Bookman*, XXXVIII (15 August 1966), 673.

Johnson, Ronald. "Letters to Walt Whitman," *Poetry*, CVIII (June 1966), 152-161. [Ten "letters" in verse.]

Johnston, Richard J. H. "Walt Whitman Stirs up a War: Brooklyn and Nicaragua at Swords' Points over a Purloined Plaque," *New York Times*, 18 March 1961.

Jones, Joseph. "Emerson and Whitman 'Down Under': Their Reception in Australia and New Zealand," *Emerson Society Quarterly*, No. 42 (I Quarter 1966), 35-46.

Kahn, Sholom J. "Classics in Words and Pictures," *Jerusalem Post*, 16 June 1961, p. vi. [Review of Gay Wilson Allen, *Walt Whitman*.]

————. "Stephen Crane and Whitman: A Possible Source for 'Maggie,'" *Walt Whitman Review*, VII (December 1961), 71-77.

————. "Whitman in Israel," *Long-Islander*, 25 May 1961, Section III, p. 1.

————. "Whitman's Allegorical Lyricism," in *Studies in English Language and Literature*. Editedby Alice Shalvi and A. A. Mendilow. Jerusalem: Mages Press of the Hebrew University, [1966.]

Kamei, Shunsuke. "Emerson, Whitman, and the Japanese in the Meiji Era (1868-1912)," *Emerson Society Quarterly*, No. 29 (IV Quarter 1962), 28-32.

————. "Takeo Arishima's Two-Day Lecture on Whitman and His Suicide," *Walt Whitman Birthplace Bulletin*, IV (January 1961), 3-7.

Kanes, Martin. "Whitman, Gide and Bazalgette: An International Encounter," *Comparative Literature*, XIV (Fall 1962), 341-355.

Katzman, Allen. "Walt Whitman and the Common Man," *American Dialog*, II (October-November 1965), 9-10.

Keenan, Randall. *The Major Poetry of Walt Whitman*. New York: Monarch Press, Inc., 1965. 144 pp.

Kilby, James A. "Walt Whitman's 'Trippers and Askers,'" *American Notes & Queries*, IV (November 1965), 37-39.

Kiley, John Francis. "Whitman as Player," *Nassau Review*, I (Spring 1965), 80. [Poem]

Kimball, William J. "'O Captain! My Captain!': Untypical Walt Whitman," *Literary Criterion* (University of Mysore, India), VI (1965), 44-47.

Kneiger, Bernard. "The Compassion of Walt Whitman," *Chicago Jewish Forum*, XXI (Winter 1962-63), 144-147.

Komroff, Manuel. "Walt Whitman: The Singer and the Chains," *Long Island University Journal*, I (June 1966), 8-17.

————. *Walt Whitman: The Singer and the Chains.* [Westwood, N. J.: Kindle Press, 1966.] 19 pp. Privately printed.

————. "Whitman's Clear Vision of the Magic in Man," *The Long-Islander*, No. 48 (1965), Section II, pp. 4-5.

Krause, Sydney. "Whitman's Yawping Bird as Comic Defense," *Bulletin of the New York Public Library*, LXVIII (June 1964), 347-360.

Kreuter, Kent K. "The Literary Response to Science, Technology, and Industrialism: Studies in the Thought of Hawthorne, Melville, Whitman, and Twain." Ph.D. dissertation, Wisconsin, 1963.

Kuhn, John G. "Whitman's Artistry: 'Then to Reproduce All in My Own Forms,' " *Walt Whitman Review*, VIII (September 1962), 51-63.

Kupferberg, Herbert. "Walt Whitman's Single Shot at Off-Broadway," *New York Herald Tribune*, 19 January 1966. [Review of "Will Geer's Americana," produced by ANTA at the Theatre de Lys, 18 January 1966.]

Landgren, Marchal E. "George C. Cox: Whitman's Photographer," *Walt Whitman Review*, IX (March 1963), 11-15, 23, 24.

Lansdale, Nelson. "Walt Whitman Worked Here," *Ford Times*, LVII (January 1964), 22-24. [On Walt Whitman House, Camden, N. J.]

Lape, Fred; Bancroft, Raymond M.; and Grant, Rena V., "Touch of the Poet," *Harper's Magazine*, CCXXII (February 1961), 8. [Letters to the Editor concerning "Wood Odors," *Harper's Magazine*, December 1960.]

LaRue, Robert. "Whitman's Sea: Large Enough for Moby Dick," *Walt Whitman Review*, XII (September 1966), 51-59.

Lasser, Michael L. "Sex and Sentimentality in Whitman's Poetry," *Emerson Society Quarterly*, No. 43 (II Quarter 1966), 94-97.

Law, Richard A. "The Respiration Motif in 'Song of Myself,'" *Walt Whitman Review*, X. (December 1964), 92-97.

Leary, Lewis. "Many Walt Whitmans, Not One?" *Walt Whitman Review*, VIII (September 1962), 68-69. [Review of Roy Harvey Pearce, *Whitman: A Collection of Critical Essays*.]

————. "Whitman's Early Writings," *Walt Whitman Review*, IX (September 1963), 69-70. [Review of Walt Whitman, *The Early Poems and the Fiction*, edited by Thomas L. Brasher.]

Lee, Brian. Review of *The Presence of Walt Whitman*, edited by R. W. B. Lewis; *Leaves of Grass: Facsimile Edition of the 1860 Text*, with an introduction by Roy Harvey Pearce; Douglas Grant, *Walt Whitman and His English Admirers*; and Richard Chase, *Walt Whitman*, *Modern Language Review*, LVIII (July 1963), 418-420.

LeWinter, Oswald. "Whitman's 'Lilacs,'" *Walt Whitman Review*, X (March 1964), 10-14.

Lewis, R. W. B. "The Aspiring Clown," in *Learners and Discerners: A Newer Criticism*, edited by Robert Scholes. Charlottesville: University Press of Virginia, 1964, pp. 63-108.

————, ed. *The Presence of Walt Whitman: Selected Papers from the English Institute*. New York and London: Columbia University Press, 1962. xvi, 215 pp.

Lid, Richard W. Review of *The Correspondence of Walt Whitman*, Vols. I and II, *This World* (San Francisco Chronicle), 3 September 1961, p. 26.

Lindeman, Jack. "Walt Whitman, My Contemporary," *American Dialog*, II (October-November 1965), 8-9.

Lindfors, Berndt. "Whitman's 'When I Heard the Learn'd Astronomer,'" *Walt Whitman Review,* X (March 1964), 19-21.

Little, William A. "Walt Whitman and the Nibelungenlied," *PMLA,* LXXX (December 1965), 562-570.

Lombard, C. M. "Whitman on French Romanticism," *Walt Whitman Review,* XII (June 1966), 41-43.

Lopez Amabilis, Manuel. "Walt Whitman," *Revue de la Universidad de Yacatan,* V (July-August 1963), 103-118. [In Spanish]

Lowenfels, Walter. "Whitman on Bruno," *Walt Whitman Review,* IX (June 1963), 42-43.

―――. "Whitman's Many Loves," *Olympia* (Paris), No. 4 (April 1963), pp. 26-32.

Lynn, Kenneth S. "Whitman's Civil War," *Christian Science Monitor,* 16 May 1963. [Review of Floyd Stovall, editor, *Prose Works 1892, Volume I: Specimen Days;* and Thomas L. Brasher, editor, *The Early Poems and the Fiction.*]

Mabbott, Thomas O. "Comprehensive Reader's Leaves of Grass," *Walt Whitman Review,* XI (June 1965), 55-56. [Review of Walt Whitman, *Leaves of Grass, Comprehensive Reader's Edition,* edited by Harold W. Blodgett and Sculley Bradley.]

―――. Review of *The Correspondence of Walt Whitman* Vols. I and II, *American Literature,* XXXIV (March 1962), 123-124.

―――. "Whitman's 'Song of Myself,' XXIV, 19," *Explicator,* V (April 1947), 43.

Madden, Richard L. "Fight to Save Print Shop Where Whitman Set 'Leaves of Grass,'" *New York Herald Tribune,* 26 November 1961.

Magee, John D. "Whitman's Cosmofloat," *Walt Whitman Review*, X(June 1964), 43-46.

Malin, Stephen D. " 'A Boston Ballad' and the Boston Riot," *Walt Whitman Review*, IX (September 1963), 51-57.

Malone, Walter Karl. "Parallels to Hindu and Taoist Thought in Walt Whitman," *Dissertation Abstracts*, XXV (1965), 4689-4690. [Temple University]

Marcus, Mordecai. "Walt Whitman and Emily Dickinson," *Personalist*, XLIII (Autumn 1963), 479-514.

Martin, Edward A. "Whitman's 'A Boston Ballad (1845),' " *Walt Whitman Review*, XI (September 1965), 61-69.

Martz, Louis L. "Whitman and Dickinson: Two Aspects of Self," *The Poem of the Mind: Essays on Poetry/English and American.* New York: Oxford University Press, 1966, pp. 82-104.

Marx, Leo. "*Democratic Vistas*: Notes for a Discussion of Whitman and the Problem of Democratic (Mass?) Culture in America," *Emerson Society Quarterly,* No. 22 (I Quarter 1961), 12-15.

Mason, Madeline. "America's Poet," *John O'London's*, V (6 July 1961), 12. [Review of *The Correspondence of Walt Whitman*, Vols. I and II.]

Mason, Philip P. "Whitman's Civil War: A Review," *Walt Whitman Review*, VII (June 1961), 37. [Review of Walter Lowenfels, *Walt Whitman's Civil War*.]

Mayfield, John. "John Quincy Adams, Walt Whitman, Charles E. Feinberg, William White, and Joseph Ishill," *The Courier* (Syracuse University Library Associates), No. 11 (September 1961), 10-11. [Review of Walt Whitman, *The People and John Quincy Adams*.]

Mazzaro, Jerome L. "Whitman's Democratic Vistas: The Vast

General Principle and Underlying Unity," *Walt Whitman Review*, VIII (December 1962), 89-90.

McAleer, John J. "Whitman and Goethe: More on the 'Van Rensellaer' Letter," *Walt Whitman Review*, VIII (December 1962), 83-85.

McClary, Ben Harris. "Burroughs to Whitman on Emerson: An Unpublished Letter," *Emerson Society Quarterly*, No. 43 (II Quarter 1966), 67-68.

McCurdy, Frances. Review of Gay Wilson Allen, *Walt Whitman As Man, Poet, and Legend*, *Quarterly Journal of Speech*, XLVIII (April 1962), 210.

McCurley, Bob. "Shirley Jones Rated as Whitman Choice," *Camden Courier-Post*, 16 November 1962.

McElderry, B. R., Jr. "Poetry and Religion: A Parallel in Whitman and Arnold," *Walt Whitman Review*, VIII (December 1962), 80-83.

————. "Robert Penn Warren and Whitman," *Walt Whitman Review*, VIII (December 1962), 91.

McLeod, A. L. "Walt Whitman in Australia," *Walt Whitman Review*, VII (June 1961), 23-35.

————. *Walt Whitman in Australia and New Zealand: A Record of His Reception*. Sydney: Wentworth Press, 1964. 161 pp. Mimeographed.

McNamara, Eugene. Review of Walter Lowenfels, *Walt Whitman's Civil War*, *America*, LIV (21 January 1961), 529.

McWhiney, Grady. Review of Walter Lowenfels, *Walt Whitman's Civil War*, *New York Herald Tribune Lively Arts and Book Review*, 9 April 1961, p. 34.

Mead, Willard. Review of Gilbert Highet, *The Powers of Poetry*, *Walt Whitman Birthplace Bulletin*, IV (April 1961), 13.

Meliado, Mariolina. "La Fortuna di Walt Whitman in Italia," *Studi Americani*, VII (1961), 43-76.

Meltzer, Milton. See Harding, Walter.

Mendelson, Maurice O. *Life and Work of Whitman*. Moscow: Scientific Publishing House, 1965. 368 pp. [In Russian]

———. "The Poetry of the Civil War in the U.S.A.," *Voprosi Literatury* [Problems in Literature], No. 2 (February 1962), 155-169. [In Russian]

———. "The Poetry of the Two Camps in the Civil War," in *Problems in the History of Literature of the U.S.A.*, edited by G. P. Zlobin. Moscow, 1964, pp. 156-204. [In Russian]

Mengeling, Marvin E. "Whitman and Ellison: Older Symbols in a Modern Mainstream," *Walt Whitman Review*, XII (September 1966), 67-70.

Metzger, Charles R. *Thoreau and Whitman: A Study of Their Esthetics*. Seattle: University of Washington Press, 1961.

Michel, Pierre. Review of Roger Asselineau, *The Evolution of Walt Whitman: The Creation of a Personality, Critical Quarterly*, III (Summer 1961), 192.

Miles, Josephine. "The Poetry of Praise," *Kenyon Review*, XXIII (Winter 1961), 104-125.

Miller, Edwin H. "Dear Father and Comrade—Unpublished Letters from Soldiers to Walt Whitman," *Long-Islander*, 24 May 1962, Section II, p. 3.

———. "Walt Whitman and Ellen Eyre," *American Literature*, XXXIII (March 1961), 64-68.

———. "Walt Whitman and Louis Fitzgerald Tasistro," *Walt Whitman Review*, VII (March 1961), 14-16.

———. "Walt Whitman as a Letter Writer," *American Book Collector*, XI (May 1961), 15-20. [From the introduction to Walt Whitman, *The Correspondence*, Vol. I.]

————. "Walt Whitman As a Lobbyist," *Yale University Library Gazette*, XXV (January 1961), 134-136.

————, ed. *Walt Whitman: The Correspondence*. Vol. I: 1842-1867; Vol. 2: 1868-1875. New York University Press, 1961.

————. "A Whitman Letter to Hiram J. Ramsdell," *Walt Whitman Review*, X(December 1964), 97-98.

Miller, F. DeWolfe. "He Wrote Items for *The Star*: Struggling Walt Whitman Had Press Agent's Skill," *Sunday Star* (Washington, D.C.), 30 July 1961, p. C-3.

————. "Introduction" to Drum-Taps (1865) and Sequel to Drum-Taps (1865-6). Gainesville, Fla.: Scholars' Facsimiles and Reprints, 1963.

————. "Malcolm Cowley Edits the First Leaves," *Walt Whitman Review*, VII (June 1961), 35-36. [Review of Malcolm Cowley, *Walt Whitman's Leaves of Grass: The First (1855) Edition.*]

————. "New Glimpses of Walt Whitman in 1886," *Tennessee Studies in Literature*, VIII (1963), 71-80.

————. "A Note on Memoranda," *Walt Whitman Review*, IX (September 1963), 67-68.

————. "The Reception of Whitman's Correspondence," *Walt Whitman Review*, IX (June 1963), 27-30.

————. Review of Gay Wilson Allen, *Walt Whitman As Man, Poet, and Legend, American Literature*, XXXIV (November 1962), 423-424.

————. "Whitman Letters Reveal Him," *Washington Post*, 9 July 1961. [Review of *The Correspondence of Walt Whitman*, Vols. I and II.]

————. "Whitman Tally, Put at Random," Studies in Honor of John C. Hodges and Alvin Thaler. Special Number,

Tennessee Studies in Literature. Knoxville: The University of Tennessee Press, 1961, pp. 151-161.

―――. "Whitman's Letters Collected," *Southern Observer,* VIII (September 1961), 139-140. [Review of *The Correspondence of Walt Whitman,* Vols. I and II.]

―――. "Whitman's 16.4 Diary," *American Book Collector,* XI (May 1961), 21-24.

Miller, Henry. "Walt Whitman," in *Stand Still Like the Hummingbird.* New York: New Directions, 1962, pp. 107-110.

Miller, James E., Jr. "Notes for an Autobiography," *Walt Whitman Review,* IX (December 1963), 90-92. [Review of Walt Whitman, *Prose Works 1892: Volume I, Specimen Days,* edited by Floyd Stovall.]

―――. Review of Walt Whitman, *Leaves of Grass: Facsimile Edition of the 1860 Text, College English,* XXIII (January 1962), 323.

―――. Review of Walt Whitman, *The Correspondence: Volume III, 1876-1885,* edited by Edwin Haviland Miller; and *Prose Works 1892: Volume II, Collect and Other Prose,* edited by Floyd Stovall, *American Literature,* XXVI (November 1964), 371-372.

―――. Karl Shapiro, and Bernice Slote. *Start with the Sun: Studies in the Whitman Tradition.* Lincoln: University of Nebraska Press, 1963. viii, 260 pp. Paperback. [Reprint of the 1960 *Start with the Sun: Studies in Cosmic Poetry.*]

―――. "The Mysticism of Whitman: Suggestions for a Seminar Discussion," *Emerson Society Quarterly,* No. 22 (I Quarter 1961), 15-18.

―――. "The Several Selves of Whitman," *Prairie Schooner,* XXXVI (Fall 1962), 280-282. [Review of *The Correspondence of Walt Whitman,* Vols. I and II.]

————. *Walt Whitman*. Twayne's United States Authors Series, No. 20. New York: Twayne Publishers, Inc., 1962. 188 pp.

————, ed. *Whitman's 'Song of Myself'—Origin, Growth, Meaning*. New York, Toronto: Dodd, Mead & Company, 1964. viii, 203 pp. Paperback.

Miller, Perry. Review of *The Correspondence of Walt Whitman*, Vols. I and II, *Christian Science Monitor*, 20 July 1961, p. 5.

————. "Whitman Papers—The Task Begins," *Christian Science Monitor*, 20 July 1961. [Review of *The Correspondence of Walt Whitman*, Vols. I and II.]

Monteiro, George. "A New Whitman Letter," *Walt Whitman Review*, XI (December 1965), 102-103.

Montesi, Albert J. Review of *The Correspondence of Walt Whitman*, Vols. I and II, *Manuscripts*, VII (July 1963), 122.

Moore, William L. *Walt Whitman's Leaves of Grass*. Prose Versions and annotations. Japanese translations by Kazuko Okamoto. Tokyo: Taibum-do, 1963. 30 pp.

Mordell, Albert. Review of Horace Traubel, *With Walt Whitman in Camden*, Vol. V. *Pennsylvania Magazine of History and Biography*, LXXXIX (April 1965), 252-254.

Morgan, Edwin. Review of Geoffrey Dutton, *Whitman*, *Review of English Studies*, XIV (February 1963), 102-103.

Moult, Thomas. Review of Malcolm Cowley, ed., *Walt Whitman's Leaves of Grass: The First (1855) Edition*, *Poetry Review*, LII (July-September 1961), 173.

Murciaux, Christian. "Walt Whitman, Poète et Prophète," *Revue des deux Mondes*, 15 November 1962, pp. 182-199.

Murphy, Robert Cushman. *Fish-Shape Paumanok: Nature and*

Man on Long Island. Philadelphia: The American Philosophical Society, 1964. ix. 67 pp.

————. "Whitman—Through a Naturalist's Eyes," *Long-Islander,* No. 48 (1965), Section II, pp. 4-5.

Nabeshima, Noriko. "Walt Whitman in Japan," *Studies in English Literature,* XLI (1965), 47-57.

Nabeshima, Yoshihiro. "On Whitman's 'When Lilacs Last in the Dooryard Bloom'd,'" *Studies in Arts and Culture* (Ochanomizu University), XIV (March 1961), 25-46.

Nambiar, O. K. *Walt Whitman and Yoga.* Bangalore, India: Jeevan Publications, 1966, xii, 183 pp.

Nandakumar, Prema. "Whitman's 'Out of the Cradle,'" *Literary Criterion* (Mysore, India), V (1962), 79-84.

Nardin, James T. Review of Floyd Stovall, *Walt Whitman: Representative Selections, College English,* XXIII (April 1962), 606.

Neilson, Kenneth P. "Toward a Walt Whitman Music Society: A Prospectus," *Walt Whitman Review,* XII (March 1966), 19-22.

————. "Walt Whitman and the Civil War Centennial," *Walt Whitman Birthplace Bulletin,* IV (April 1961), 15.

Nist, John. "Two American Poets and a Spider," *Walt Whitman Birthplace Bulletin,* IV (January 1961), 8-11. [Whitman and Emily Dickinson's use of the spider.]

Oliver, Egbert S. "Walt Whitman and Asia," *Emerson Society Quarterly,* No. 22 (I Quarter 1961), 18-20.

————. "Walt Whitman's 'Passage to India,'" " 'The Seas Are All Cross'd': Whitman and World Freedom," "Walt Whitman and Asia," in *Studies in American Literature: Whitman, Emerson, Melville and Others.* Ram Nagar, New Delhi: Eurasia Publishing House (P) Ltd., 1965, pp. 116-138.

39

Page, A. F. "A Whitman Portrait," *Walt Whitman Review*, VII (June 1961), 36. [Review of Antonio Frasconi, *A Whitman Portrait: Woodcuts.*]

Paul, Sherman. *Louis Sullivan: An Architect in American Thought.* Englewood Cliffs, N. J.: Prentice-Hall, 1962. [Whitman mentioned throughout the book.]

Paxton, Claire. "Unamuno's Indebtedness to Whitman," *Walt Whitman Review*, IX (March 1963), 16-19.

Pearce, Roy Harvey. *The Continuity of American Poetry.* Princeton University Press, 1961. ["Song of Myself," pp. 69-83; "Whitman," pp. 164-174.]

————. Review of Roger Asselineau, *The Evolution of Walt Whitman: The Creation of a Personality, Modern Language Notes,* LXXVI (December 1961), 899-900.

————. Review of Walt Whitman, *Leaves of Grass: Comprehensive Reader's Edition,* edited by Harold W. Blodgett and Sculley Bradley, *English Language Notes,* III (March 1966), 231-233.

————, ed. *Whitman: A Collection of Critical Reviews.* Englewood Cliffs, N. J.: Prentice-Hall, Inc., 1962.

————. "Whitman Justified: The Poet in 1860," *Minnesota Review*, I (April 1961), 261-294.

Peters, Robert L. "Edmund Gosse's Two Whitmans," *Walt Whitman Review*, XI (March 1965), 19-21.

Pfeifer, Edward J. "The Theory of Evolution and Whitman's 'Passage to India,'" *Emerson Society Quarterly*, No. 42 (I Quarter 1966), 31-35.

Poenicke, Klaus. " 'The Test of Death and Night'—Pose und bewältigte Wirklichkeit in Whitmans Leaves of Grass," *Festschrift für Walter Hubner*, edited by Dieter Riesner and Helmut Gneuss. Berlin: Schmidt, 1964, pp. 239-266.

Posey, M. N. Review of Walt Whitman, *The Correspondence:*

Vol. III, 1876-1855, edited by Edwin Haviland Miller, *South Atlantic Quarterly*, LXIV (Winter 1965), 150.

Preuschen, Karl Adalbert. "Zur entstehung der neuen Lyrik in Amerika: Walt Whitman: Song of Myself (1. Fassung)," *Jahrubuch fur Amerikastudien*, VIII (1963), 148-170.

Puga, Raul E. "Walt Whitman: El Profeta de Norteamerica," *Magazine de Novedades* (Mexico, D.F.), 29 July 1962, p. 10.

Rand, George I. "Walt Whitman in Rumania," *Emerson Society Quarterly*, No. 43 (II Quarter 1966), 113-116.

————. "Tennyson's Gift to Walt Whitman—A New Letter," *Emerson Society Quarterly*, No. 24 (III Quarter 1961), pp. 106-109.

Reeves, Paschal. "The Silhouette of the State in Democratic Vistas—Hegelian or Whitmanian?" *Person*, XLIII (July 1962), 374-382.

Reiss, Edmund. "Whitman's Debt to Animal Magnetism," *PMLA*, LXXVIII (1963), 80-88.

Resnick, Nathan. "Is Whitman's Message Applicable Today?" *Long-Islander*, No. 48 (1965), Section II, pp. 4-5.

————. " 'The Whole Earth Enjoyable,' " *Long Island University Journal*, I (June 1966), 5-7.

Riddel, Joseph N. "Walt Whitman and Wallace Stevens: Functions of a 'Literatus,' " *South Atlantic Quarterly*, LXI (Autumn 1962), 506-520.

Riese, Teut. Review of James E. Miller, Jr., *A Critical Guide to 'Leaves of Grass,'* " *Archiv fur das Studium der neuren Sprachen*, CXCVII (1961), 209-210.

Rising, Clara. "Vistas of a Disillusioned Realist," *Walt Whitman Review*, VII (December 1961), 63-71.

Rivière, Jean. "Howells and Whitman after 1881," *Walt Whitman Review*, XII (December 1967), 97-100.

Rizzo, Patrick V. "John F. Kennedy and Whitman," *Walt Whitman Review*, X(June 1964), 42.

————. "Walt Whitman, Amateur Astronomer," *Asterisks* (Amateur Astronomers Association, New York), No. 6 (October 1964), 7-10, 13.

————. "When I Heard the Learn'd Astronomer," *Skylines* (Amateur Astronomers Association, New York City), November 1961, p. 6.

Robbins, J. Albert. "America and the Poet: Whitman, Hart Crane and Frost," *American Poetry*. London: Edwin Arnold; New York: St. Martin's Press, 1965, pp. 45-67.

Roesler, Sister Miriam Clare, O.S.F. "The Sea and Death in Walt Whitman's *Leaves of Grass*," *Dissertation Abstracts*, XXIV (1963), 1606.

Rogers, Fred B. "Walt Whitman: A Fardel of Admirers," *Proceedings of the New Jersey Historical Society,* LXXXIII (October 1965), 275-286.

Rosenfeld, Alvin. "The Poem as Dialogical Process: A New Reading of 'Salut au Monde!,' " *Walt Whitman Review,* X(June 1964), 34-40.

Rosenthal, Peggy .Z "Whitman Music: The Problem of Adaptation," *Books at Brown*, XX (1965), 71-97.

Rosten, Norman. "Face on the Daguerreotype: For Walt Whitman," *Long Island University Journal*, I (June 1966), 28. [Poem.]

Rotchford, Charlene M. "Walt Whitman's Modern Music," *Music Journal*, XIX (March 1961), 44, 82.

Rubin, Joseph Jay. "Whitman: Equal Rights in the Foreground," *Emerson Society Quarterly*, No. 22 (I Quarter 1961), 20-23.

Ryan, Robert. "College Plans Walt Whitman Festival," *Sunday Herald Tribune* (New York), 16 May 1965, Section 5, pp. 1, 7.

Sachithanandan, V. "Bharati and Whitman," *Literary Criterion* (Mysore, India), V (1962), 85-94.

————. "Bharati and Whitman," *Symposium*, XIX (Fall 1965), 259-266.

Sachs, Viola. "The Poetics of Walt Whitman,' '*Przegld Humanistyczny* [Humanistic Survey], VI (1962), 45-68. [In Polish]

————. "Walt Whitman and the Orientals," *Kwartalnik Neofilologiczny* (Warsaw), IX (1962), 147-160.

Salvan, J. L. "A French View of Whitman," *Walt Whitman Review*, VI (December 1960), 74-76. [Review of Alain Bosquet, *Whitman.*]

Sayre, Robert F. Review of Walt Whitman, *Prose Works 1892: Volume I, Specimen Days; Volume II, Collect and Other Prose*, edited by Floyd Stovall; and *The Correspondence: Volume III, 1876-1885*, edited by Edwin Haviland Miller, *Journal of English and Germanic Philology*, LXIV (April 1965), 339-342.

Schiller, Andrew. "An Approach to Whitman's Metrics," *Emerson Society Quarterly*, No. 22 (I Quarter 1961), 23-25.

Schwab, Arnold T. "James Huneker on Whitman: A Newly Discovered Essay," *American Literature*, XXXVIII (May 1966), 208-218.

Schwartz, Arthur. "The Each and All of Whitman's Verse," *Emerson Society Quarterly*, No. 22 (I Quarter 1961), 25-26.

Sewell, Elizabeth. "Science and Literature," *Commonweal*, LXXXIV (13 May 1966), 218-221.

Sewell, Richard H. "Walt Whitman, John P. Hale, and the Free Democracy: An unpublished Letter," *New England Quarterly*, XXXIV (June 1961), 239-242.

Shahane, V. A. "Aspects of Walt Whitman's Symbolism," *Literary Criterion* (Mysore, India), V (1962), 72-78.

Shapiro, Karl. "Is Poetry an American Art?" *College English*, XXV (March 1964), 395-405.

Sharma, Som P. "Self, Soul, and God in 'Passage to India,'" *College English*, XXVII (February 1966), 394-399.

————. "A Study of Themes, Self, Love, War, and Death in Relationship to Form in the Poetry of Walt Whitman," *Dissertation Abstracts*, XXIV (1964), 4703-4704.

Shephard, Esther. "Whitman's Copy of George Sand's 'Consuelo,'" *Walt Whitman Review*, IX (June 1963), 34-36, 47.

Shivers, Alfred S. "Nursery Stories for Adults: II. Story of the Lazy Carpenter," Illustrated by Donald Murray, *American Book Collector*, XVI (January 1966), 10-11.

Shuman, R. Baird. "Clarence Darrow's Estimate of Whitman," *Walt Whitman Review*, VIII (December 1962), 86-87.

Shyre, Paul. "A Whitman Portrait: A Dramatic Narrative in Two Acts," *Nassau Review*, I (Spring 1965), 19-79.

Silver, Rollo G., ed. Fourth Annual Special Whitman Page, *The Long-Islander,* 30 May 1963, Section 2, pp. 8, 10.

Skipp, Francis E. "Whitman and Shelley: A Possible Source for 'The Sleepers,'" *Walt Whitman Review*, XI (September 1965), 69-74.

————. "Whitman's 'Lucifer': A Footnote to 'The Sleepers,'" *Walt Whitman Review*, XI (June 1965), 52-53.

Slote, Bernice. "Willa Cather and Walt Whitman," *Walt Whitman Review*, XII (March 1966), 3-5.

Smith, Harriet. "Walt Whitman and Rabindranath Tagore: Precursors of Universal Man," *Visvaghara TI Quarterly,* XXIX (1963-64), 4-14.

Sodré, Alita. "Consideraçoes sōbre Walt Whitman," *Kriterion* (Minas Gerais), Nos. 55-56 (January-June 1961), 207-214.

Spector, Robert D. "In Praise of the Innermost Self," *Saturday Review,* XLVIII (27 February 1965), 48. [Review of *Leaves of Grass: Comprehensive Reader's Edition,* edited by Harold W. Blodgett and Sculley Bradley.]

Spencer, Benjamin T. " 'Beautiful Blood and Beautiful Brain': Whitman and Poe," *Emerson Society Quarterly,* No. 35 (II Quarter 1964), 45-49.

Stavrou, C. N. *Whitman and Nietzsche: A Comparative Study of Their Thought.* Chapel Hill: The University of North Carolina Press, 1964. xiii, 232 pp.

Steensma, Robert C. "Whitman and General Custer," *Walt Whitman Review,* X (June 1964), 41-42.

Stein, William Bysshe. "Whitman: The Divine Ferryman," *Walt Whitman Review,* VIII (June 1962), 27-33.

Stewart, Randall. *The Literature of the United States,* II. New York: Scott, Foresman, 1966. Third Edition, pp. 152. [Contains explication of "Passage to India."]

Stoller, Leo. Review of Roger Asselineau, *The Evolution of Walt Whitman, Science & Society,* XXVI (Summer 1962), 345-348.

Stovall, Floyd. "On Editing Walt Whitman's Papers," *Mississippi Quarterly,* XV (Summer 1962), 120-125.

————, ed. Walt Whitman: *Prose Works 1892: Volume I: Specimen Days.* With Notes. *The Collected Writings of Walt Whitman.* New York University Press, 1963.

————. Review of Roger Asselineau, *The Evolution of Walt*

Whitman, American Literature, XXXV (March 1963), 96-97.

―――. Review of V. K. Chari, *Whitman in the Light of Vedantic Mysticism: An Interpretation, American Literature* XXXVII (January 1966), 486-487.

―――. "Whitman's Prose: The Comparison to 'Leaves of Grass,' " *Long-Islander,* 28 May 1964, Section III, p. 1.

Strohl, Beverly L. "An Interpretation of 'Out of the Cradle,' " *Walt Whitman Review,* X (December 1964), 83-87.

Sullivan, Arthur M. "Incident at Sunken Meadow," *Nassau Review,* I (Spring 1965), 99-100. [Poem.]

Sullivan, Edward E., Jr. "Thematic Unfolding in Whitman's 'Drum Taps,' " *Emerson Society Quarterly,* No. 31 (II Quarter 1963), Part 2, pp. 42-45.

Summerhayes, Don. "Joyce's 'Ulysses' and Whitman's 'Self': A Query," *Wisconsin Studies in Contemporary Literature,* IV (Spring-Summer 1963), 216-224.

Talbot, N. C. "Walt Whitman, the Monster and the Critic," in *Proceedings of the Ninth Congress of the Australasian Universities' Languages and Literature Association,* 19-26 August 1964. Melbourne: University of Melbourne, 1964, pp. 61-62.

Tannenbaum, Earl. "Pattern in Whitman's 'Song of Myself'— A Summary and a Supplement," *College Language Association Journal,* VI (September 1962), 44-49.

Tanner, James T. F. "The Lamarckian Theory of Progress in *Leaves of Grass,*" *Walt Whitman Review,* IX (March 1963), 3-11.

―――. "The Superman in *Leaves of Grass,*" *Walt Whitman Review,* XI (December 1965), 85-100.

―――. "Walt Whitman: Curious Eclectic," *The Long-Islander,* 28 May 1964, Section III, p. 1.

————. "Walt Whitman—Poet of Lamarckian Evolution." Ph.D. dissertation, Texas Tech., 1965.

————. "Whitman's Reception 'Down Under,' " *Walt Whitman Review*, XI (June 1965), 54. [Review of A. L. McLeod, *Walt Whitman in Australia and New Zealand*.]

Tanner, Tony. "An Introduction to the Modern World," *Time and Tide* (London), XLII (16 March 1961), 430-431. [Review-article on *Leaves of Grass*.]

Tanselle, G. Thomas. "Whitman's Short Stories: Another Reprint," *Papers of the Bibliographical Society of America*, LVI (I Quarter 1962), 115.

Teller, Walter. "Speaking of Books: Whitman at Timber Creek," *The New York Times Book Review*, 10 April 1966, pp. 2, 31.

Thompson, Ernest. "Whitman's Friend Relates Poet's Inner Thoughts," *Ada (Oklahoma) Evening News*, 11 January 1965. [Review of Horace Traubel, *With Walt Whitman in Camden*, Vol. V.]

Thompson, Leslie. "Promise of America in Whitman and Thomas Wolfe: 'Song of Myself' and 'You Can't Go Home Again,' " *Walt Whitman Review*, XII (June 1966), 27-34.

Thorp, Willard. "Some Whitman Firsts at Princeton—And How They Got There," *Long-Islander*, 28 May 1964, Section III, p. 1.

Thorpe, Dan. "Whitman Letters in New Edition," *Sunday Star* (Washington, D.C.), 2 July 1961.

Tichy, Francois. "Exemplary," *Mainstream*, XIV (September 1961), 61-64. [Review of Walter Lowenfels, *Walt Whitman's Civil War*.]

Toperoff, Sam. "Reconciliation of Polarity in Whitman's

'Drum Taps,'" *Emerson Society Quarterly*, No. 31 (II Quarter 1963), Part 2, pp. 45-47.

―――. "Whitman's Raft Metaphor," *Emerson Society Quarterly*, No. 38 (I Quarter 1965), pp. 130-132.

Toruno, Juãn Felipe. "Walt Whitman, Biblico, Futurista Poeta de America," *Journal of Inter-American Studies*, IV (January 1962), 23-31.

Traubel, Horace. *With Walt Whitman in Camden: April 8-September 14, 1889*. (Volume V). Carbondale: Southern Illinois University Press, 1964. xiii, 524 pp.

Turner, Arlin. Review of *Leaves of Grass: Comprehensive Reader's Edition*, edited by Harold W. Blodgett and Sculley Bradley, *South Atlantic Quarterly*, LXIV (Autumn 1965), 576.

Tuttle, Robert C. "The Identity of Walt Whitman: Motive, Theme, and Form in *Leaves of Grass*." Ph.D. dissertation, Washington, 1965.

Undurraga, Antonio de. "Walt Whitman y el hombre total," *La Semana*, No. 70 (el 21 de enero de 1961), 1, 13, 16.

Viguers, R. H. Review of James Daugherty, *Walt Whitman's America*, *Horn Book*, XLI (February 1965), 62.

Walker, John. "Eakins in Washington," *Art in America*, XLIX (1961), 57-59.

Wankhade, Manohar Namedeo. "Walt Whitman and Tantrism: A Comparative Study." Ph.D. dissertation, Florida, 1965.

Waterman, Arthur E. "A Criticism of 'When Lilacs Last in the Dooryard Bloom'd,'" *Walt Whitman Review*, VIII (1962), 64-68.

Warfel, Harry R. "Collecting Walt Whitman," *American Book Collector*, XI (May 1961), 25.

————. "A Seminar in *Leaves of Grass*," *Emerson Society Quarterly*, No. 22 (I Quarter 1961), 27-28.

————. "Walt's Tribute to Lincoln," *South Atlantic Bulletin* (South Atlantic Modern Language Association), XXX (May 1965), 1-3.

Waskow, Howard J. *Whitman: Explorations in Form*. University of Chicago Press, 1966.

Watt, Olivia B. "Humanitarianism in Walt Whitman," *Walt Whitman Review*, X (September 1964), 60-67.

Wermuth, Paul C. "Letter to Walt Whitman," *Emerson Society Quarterly*, No. 22 (I Quarter 1961), 1. [Poem.]

Westbrook, Perry D. *The Greatness of Man: An Essay on Dostoyevsky and Whitman*. New York, London: Thomas Yoseloff, 1961.

Westlake, Neda M. "Walt Whitman at the University of Pennsylvania," *Long-Islander*, 28 May 1964, Section III, p. 1.

Whicher, Stephen, and Ahnebrink, eds. "Walt Whitman," in *Twelve American Poets*. New York: Oxford University Press, 1961, pp. 42-55.

————. "Whitman's Awakening to Death: Toward a Biographical Reading of 'Out of the Cradle Endlessly Rocking,'" *Studies in Romanticism* (Boston University), I (Autumn 1961), 9-28.

White, Gertrude M. "The Poem of the Mind: Review," *Walt Whitman Review*, XII (September 1966), 71-72. [Review of fifth chapter ("Whitman and Dickinson: Two Aspects of Self") of Louis L. Martz, *The Poem of The Mind: Essays on Poetry/English and American.*]

————. "Poetry as Cultural History," *Walt Whitman Review*, VIII (March 1962), 20-22. [Review of Roy Harvey Pearce, *The Continuity of American Poetry.*]

————. "Whitman in Pictures," *American Book Collector* IX (May 1961), 3. [Review of Gay Wilson Allen, *Walt Whitman.*]

White, William. "Complete Poems & Prose Inscribed to Traubel," *Walt Whitman Review*, XII (September 1966), 73-74.

————. "The Editions of *Leaves of Grass*," "The First Important Whitman Letter," and "A 'Leaves of Grass' Never Published," *Long-Islander*, 30 May 1963, Section II, pp. 8, 10.

————. ["Error in Whitman Portrait"], *Nimatour* (South Pasadena), No. XVII (April 1965), pp. 3-4.

————. "Fanny Fern to Walt Whitman: An Unpublished Letter," *American Book Collector*, XI (May 1961), 9. [Illustration on p. 8.]

————. "The First (1855) 'Leaves of Grass': How Many Copies?" *Papers of the Bibliographical Society of America*, LVII (III Quarter 1963), 352-354.

————. "First Whitman Paperback," *Walt Whitman Review*, XII (March 1966), 23-24.

————. $400 for the Brooklyn Freeman?" *Walt Whitman Review*, VII (December 1961), [80.]

————. "The Hempstead Tragedy," *American Book Collector*, XI (May 1961), 27. [Illustration on p. 26.]

————. "Herbert Gilchrist's Pen & Ink Whitman," *Walt Whitman Review*, XI (December 1965), 105-106.

————. "How to Become Eminent; or, Life among the Feinberg MSS," *Walt Whitman Birthplace Bulletin*, IV (July 1961), 3-7.

————. "In Whitman's Hand," *American Notes & Queries*, II (February 1964), 86.

————. "Literary Snooping in the Feinberg Collection," *Hobbies*, LXVII (April 1962), 110-111, 117. [Reprinted from *Walt Whitman Birthplace Bulletin.*]

————. "Morley on Whitman: Inedité," *American Notes & Queries*, IV (May 1966), 132-133.

————. "MS of 'How I Get Around,'" *Walt Whitman Review*, X (December 1964), 103-104.

————. " 'Nationalism': Unpublished Whitman?" *American Notes & Queries*, I (January 1963), 67-68.

————. "A Nation's Poems: An Unpublished Fragment," *Walt Whitman Review*, XII (December 1966), 103. [Plate on p. 104.]

————. "Oscar Wilde on Whitman: A Review," *Walt Whitman Review*, VIII (December 1962), 93-94. [Review of *The Letters of Oscar Wilde.*]

————. "The Poet and Mrs. Fels," *Walt Whitman Review*, X (September 1964), 79-80.

————. "Preface to Democratic Vistas," *Walt Whitman Review*, IX (September 1963), 71, 72.

————. "Priestley in Texas," *The American Book Collector*, XIII (March 1963), 7.

————. Review of *The Correspondence of Walt Whitman*, Vols. I and II, *Bulletin of Bibliography*, XXIII (May-August 1961), 102.

————. "Robinson Jeffer's Space," *Personalist*, XLIV (Spring 1963), 175-179. [Compares Jeffers with Whitman.]

————. "A Russian Anthology of American Poetry," *Walt Whitman Review* IX (September 1963), 68-69.

————. "Some Uncollected Whitman Journalism," *Emerson Society Quarterly*, No. 33 (IV Quarter 1963), 84-90.

————. "A 'Strange Coincidence' in Walt Whitman," *Walt*

Whitman Review, XI (December 1965), 100-102. [Review of Henry M. Christman, *Walt Whitman's New York.*]

———. "A Thousand and One MSS by Walt Whitman," *Orient/West* (Tokyo), VIII (July-August 1963), 69-80.

———. "Traubel the Fifth," *Walt Whitman Review,* X (December 1964), 100-101. [Review of Horace Traubel, *With Walt Whitman in Camden,* Vol. V.]

———. "Traubel's 'With Walt Whitman in Camden,'" *Antiquarian Bookman,* XXXV (4-11 January 1965), 13. [Addenda to "With Walt Whitman in Camden: A Bibliographical Note," *Antiquarian Bookman,* XXXIV (30 November 1964), 2260-2261.]

———. "Trial Lines for the 1855 Leaves?" *Walt Whitman Review,* VII (September 1961), 60.

———. "An Unpublished Whitman Notebook for 'Lilacs,'" *Modern Language Quarterly,* XXIV (June 1963), 177-180.

———. "Walt: No Omnibus Driver," *Walt Whitman Review,* XI (December 1965), 105.

———. "Walt Whitman and Lafayette," *Tradition,* IV (November 1961), 32-35.

———. "Walt Whitman in 'Ideals of Life,'" *American Book Collector,* XI (May 1961), 30-31.

———. "Walt Whitman's 'Elegy,': An Early Poem?" *Notes & Queries,* n.s. IX (June 1962), 227-228.

———. Walt Whitman: "Shirval: A Tale of Jerusalem," with a note by William White. *The Daily Collegian* (Wayne State University), LIII (28 February 1963), 8.

———. "'A Week' in the Feinberg Collection," *Thoreau Society Bulletin,* No. 85 (Fall 1963), 2. [Thoreau's annotation in Whitman's copy.]

——. "Walt Whitman: Journalist," *Journalism Quarterly* XXXIX (Summer 1962), 339-346.

——. "Walt Whitman on French Cookery," *Accent on Home Economics* (Wayne State University), No. 10 (Spring 1962), 1-4.

——. "Walt Whitman's Pseudonyms," *American Notes & Queries*, IV (March 1966), 105.

——. "What is Poetry? An Early Draft," *Walt Whitman Review*, VIII (September 1962), 72.

——. "Whitmaniana," *American Book Collector*, XI (May 1961), 11-14. [Illustration on p. 10.]

——. "Whitman in Paperback," *American Book Collector*, XI (May 1961), 28-30.

——. "Whitman in Pictures," *Detroit Free Press*, 17 September 1961, Section B, p. 3. [Review of Gay Wilson Allen, *Walt Whitman.*]

——. "Whitman on American Poets: An Uncollected Piece," *English Language Notes*, I (September 1963), 42-43.

——. "Whitman Photo to William Bell Scott," *Walt Whitman Review*, XI (March 1965), 23-24.

——. "Whitman's Commonplace Book," *Walt Whitman Review*, XII (June 1966), 47-48.

——. "Whitman's Copy of Epictetus," *Walt Whitman Review*, VIII (December 1962), 95.

——. "Whitman's Death of Lincoln in Miniature and Two Paperbacks," *Walt Whitman Review*, VIII (June 1962), 44-46. [Review of Walt Whitman, *Death of Abraham Lincoln*; Walt Whitman, *Specimen Days*; and Floyd Stovall, *Walt Whitman: Representative Selections.}*

——. "Whitman's Democratic Vistas: An Unpublished

Self-Review?" *American Book Collector*, XVI (December 1965), 21.

―――. "Whitman's First 'Literary Letter," *American Literature*, XXXV (March 1963), 83-85.

―――. "Whitman's *Leaves of Grass*: Notes on the Pocketbook (1889) Edition," *Studies in Bibliography: Papers of the Bibliographical Society of the University of Virginia*, XVIII (1965), 280-281.

―――. "Whitman's Letters," *American Book Collector*, XII (April 1962), 3-4. [Review of *The Correspondence of Walt Whitman*, Vols. I and II, edited by Edwin Haviland Miller.]

―――. "Whitman's Lincoln," *American Book Collector*, XII (Summer 1962), 4. [Review of Walt Whitman, *Death of Abraham Lincoln*; Roy P. Basler, *Walt Whitman's Memoranda During the War*; and William Coyle, *The Poet and the President*.]

―――. "Whitman's Poem on the Johnstown Flood," *Emerson Society Quarterly*, No. 33 (1963), pp. 79-84.

―――. "William Douglas O'Connor in 1887," *Walt Whitman Review*, XI (June 1965), 57-58.

―――. " 'With Walt Whitman in Camden': A Bibliographical Note," *Antiquarian Bookman*, XXXIV (30 November 1964), 2260-2261.

―――. "Yearly Report to the Stockholders. . . ," *Long-Islander*, No. 48 (1965), Section II, pp. 4-5.

Willingham, J. R. Review of Roger Asselineau, *The Evolution of Walt Whitman*, Vol. II, *Library Journal*, LXXXVIII (1 January 1963), 102.

―――. Review of Walt Whitman, *AN 1855-56 Notebook*, edited by Harold W. Blodgett, *Books Abroad*, XXXV (Autumn 1961), 393-394.

————. Review of Walt Whitman, *The Early Poems and the Fiction*, edited by Thomas L. Brasher; and *Prose Works 1892: Volume I, Specimen Days*, edited by Floyd Stovall, *Library Journal*, LXXXVIII (15 May 1963), 2011.

————. Review of *The Correspondence of Walt Whitman*, Vols. I and II, *Library Journal*, LXXXVI (August 1961), 2646.

————. Review of Henry M. Christman, editor, *Walt Whitman's New York*, *Library Journal*, LXXXVIII (15 November 1963), 4376.

Woodward, Robert H. "John F. Kennedy and Whitman: Addendum," *Walt Whitman Review*, XII (June 1966), 44-45.

————. "Voyage Imagery in 'Terminus' and 'O Captain! My Captain!'" *Emerson Society Quarterly*, No. 27 (II Quarter 1962), p. 37.

————. "Walt Whitman: The White House by Moonlight," *Walt Whitman Review*, IX (June, 1963), p. 42.

Wylder, Robert C. Review of Gay Wilson Allen, *Walt Whitman As Man, Poet and Legend*, *Western Humanities Review*, XVII (Summer 1963), 290.

Wyllie, John Cook. "The Barrett Collection of Walt Whitman," *American Book Collector*, XI (May 1961), 33. [Illustration on p. 32.]

Yerbury, Grace D. "Of a City Beside a River: Whitman, Eliot, Thomas, Miller," *Walt Whitman Review*, X (September 1964), 67-73.

Yohannan, John D. "Whitman and Mysticism," *Long-Islander*, 26 May 1966, Section II, p. 5. [Review of V. K. Chari, *Whitman in the Light of Vedantic Mysticism*.]

Zandvoort, R. W. Review of Douglas Grant, *Walt Whitman and His English Admirers*, *English Studies*, XLIV (1963), 75.

Zanger, Jules. "Whitman and the Influence of Space on American Literature: A Report on the Twelfth Newberry Library Conference on American Studies," *Newberry Library Bulletin,* V (December 1961), 299-314.

Zebrowski, Walter M. "Whitman in Poland," *Polish American Studies,* XIX (January-June 1962), 57-59.

Unsigned. "Annual Board Meeting [Walt Whitman Birthplace Association]," *Walt Whitman Birthplace Bulletin,* IV (July 1961), 8-9.

————."The Bird of Freedom," *Times Literary Supplement,* 2 June 1961, p. 340. [Review-essay of Roger Asselineau, *The Evolution of Walt Whitman,* and Malcolm Cowley, *Walt Whitman's Leaves of Grass: The First (1855) Edition.*]

————. "From Bolton, England," *Walt Whitman Birthplace Bulletin,* IV (July 1961), 28-29.

————. "Millholland in Whitman Show," *Walt Whitman Birthplace Bulletin,* IV (July 1961), 12.

————. "Mrs. Smith's Silver Tea," *Walt Whitman Birthplace Bulletin,* IV (July 1961), 9.

————. "Notable Gathering of Whitman Scholars," *Walt Whitman Birthplace Bulletin,* IV (July 1961), 7-8.

————. Review of *The Correspondence of Walt Whitman,* Vols. I and II, *Antiquarian Bookman,* XXVIII (7 August 1961), 458.

————. Review of Walter Lowenfels, *Walt Whitman's Civil War, English Journal,* L (May 1961), 365.

————. Review of Walter Lowenfels, *Walt Whitman's Civil War, Civil War History,* VII (September 1961), 350.

————. "Two Volumes of Whitman's Letters," *Walt Whitman Birthplace Bulletin,* IV (July 1961), 10-11.

————. "Walt in Paperback," *Walt Whitman Birthplace Bulletin*, IV (July 1961), 11. [Review of Gay Wilson Allen, *Walt Whitman.*]

————. "Walt Whitman's War," *Walt Whitman Birthplace Bulletin*, IV (July 1961), 15. [Review of Walter Lowenfels, *Walt Whitman's Civil War.*]

————. "Whitman's Memory Honored in Sweden," "More about Calamus," "Calamus in Music," "The Colyer House," *Walt Whitman Birthplace Bulletin*, IV (January 1961), 14-21.

————. "What's the Statue?" *WFLN Philadelphia Guide*, I (1 May 1961), 19. [Jo Davidson's statue near the Walt Whitman Bridge, Camden-Philadelphia.]

————. "Unpublished Whitman Poem Found in California Attic" [and] "The Newly Discovered Whitman Manuscript," *Walt Whitman Birthplace Bulletin*, IV (January 1961), 12-14.

————. "Cleanup Ordered at Whitman Home," *Camden Courier-Post*, 27 November 1962.

————. "Holloway MS in the Berg Collection," *Walt Whitman Review*, VIII (June 1962), 47.

————. "Whitman in Our Times," *Times Literary Supplement* (London), 16 February 1962, p. 106. [Review of Gay Wilson Allen, *Walt Whitman As Man, Poet, and Legend.*]

————. "O'Dowd to Whitman—Whitman to O'Dowd," *Overland* (Melbourne, Australia), No. 23 (April 1962), 8-18.

————. "Poet of 'The Modern,' " *Times Literary Supplement*, 2 November 1962, p. 840. [Review of *The Correspondence of Walt Whitman*, Vols. I and II, edited by Edwin

Haviland Miller and Roy P. Basler, *Walt Whitman's Memoranda During the War.*]

————. *Leaves of Grass: Analytic Notes and Criticism.* A Study Master Publication. New York: American R.D.M. Corporation, 1962. 60 pp.

————. "Walt Whitman," in *Picture Book of American Authors.* Visual History Series, pp. 28-29. New York: Sterling Publishing Co., 1962.

————. "Books Selected for White House," *New York Times,* 16 August 1963, pp. 1, 22-24.

————. Brief review of Roger Asselineau, *The Evolution of Walt Whitman,* Vols. I and II, *Times Literary Supplement* (London), 7 June 1963, p. 402.

————. Review of Floyd Stovall, ed., *Prose Works 1892, Volume I: Specimen Days, Long-Islander,* 30 May 1963.

————. Review of Roger Asselineau, *The Evolution of Walt Whitman,* Vol. II, *Virginia Quarterly Review,* XXXIX (Spring 1963), lviii.

————. Review of Roger Asselineau, *The Evolution of Walt Whitman,* Vol. II, *Yale Review,* LII (Spring 1963), xxviii.

————. Review of Thomas L. Brasher, ed., *The Early Poems and the Fiction, Long-Islander,* 30 May 1963.

————. Review of Walt Whitman, *The Early Poems and the Fiction,* edited by Thomas L. Brasher, *Bulletin of Bibliography,* XXIV (May-August 1963), 7.

————. "A Whitman Sculpture" [plate], *Walt Whitman Review,* IX (December 1963), 95.

————. "Writer's Progress," *Times Literary Supplement* (London), 21 June 1963, p. 456. [Review of Walt Whitman, *The Early Poems and the Fiction,* edited by Thomas

L. Brasher; and *Prose Works 1892: Volume I, Specimen Days*, edited by Floyd Stovall.]

———. "America—a Nation of Nations," Z.O.A. *House News* (Tel Aviv), IV (September-October 1964), 2.

———. "'Hegel—to Introduce': Whitman, a MS," *Walt Whitman Review*, X(June 1964), 48.

———. "A Weekend for Whitman," *Newsday* (New York), 24 May 1965, Newsday Center Section, p. 1c.

———. "[Emerson's Copy of *Leaves of Grass*]," *Research News* (University of Michigan), XV (April 1965), 9.

———. Review of Horace Traubel, *With Walt Whitman in Camden: April 8-September 14, 1889* (Volume V), *American Literature*, XXXVII (May 1965), 229.

———. Review of Horace Traubel, *With Walt Whitman in Camden: April 8-September 14, 1889* (Volume V), *Virginia Quarterly Review*, XLI (Spring 1965), liv.

———. Review of James Daugherty, *Walt Whitman's America*, *Booklist*, LXI (1 February 1965), 530.

———. Review of Walt Whitman, *Leaves of Grass: Comprehensive Reader's Edition*, edited by Harold W. Blodgett and Sculley Bradley, *Antiquarian Bookman*, XXXV (1 February 1965), 416.

———. Reviews of Walt Whitman, *Leaves of Grass: Comprehensive Reader's Edition*, edited by Harold W. Blodgett and Sculley Bradley, *Booklist*, LXI (15 April 1965), 788.

———. Reviews of Walt Whitman, *Leaves of Grass: Comprehensive Reader's Edition*, edited by Harold W. Blodgett and Sculley Bradley, *Choice: Books for College Libraries*, II (June 1965), 230.

———. Reviews of Walt Whitman, *Leaves of Grass: Com-

59

prehensive Reader's Edition, edited by Harold W. Blodgett and Sculley Bradley, *Christian Science Monitor,* LVII (11 February 1965), 7.

———. "Whitman's 'Blue Book,' and Messrs. Traubel, Lion, and Golden," *Bulletin of the New York Public Library,* LXIX (February 1965), 73.

———. "News Texts for Old Tales," *Times Literary Supplement* (London), 26 May 1966, p. 477. [Review of Walt Whitman, *Leaves of Grass: Comprehensive Reader's Edition,* edited by Harold W. Blodgett and Sculley Bradley.]